POEMS 1920-1945

For oft in midnight streets I hear
How the youthful harlot's curse
Blasts the newborn infant's ear
And blights with plagues the marriage hearse.

POEMS

1920-1945

A SELECTION

BY

ALLEN TATE

1947

EYRE & SPOTTISWOODE

LONDON

To
ALFRED AND ELIZABETH STARR

THIS BOOK IS PRINTED FOR EYRE & SPOTTISWOODE
(PUBLISHERS) LTD., 14, 15, AND 16 BEDFORD STREET,
LONDON, W.C. 2, BY T. & A. CONSTABLE LTD.,
HOPETOUN STREET, EDINBURGH

AUTHOR'S NOTE

The earliest poem in this book was written in December 1920, and it seems to me as if somebody else must have written it. In arranging the poems I have avoided the chronological order and set them out in groups, which may not make much sense to anybody else; and I am not sure I know why I think certain poems go together. At the suggestion of Mr. Willard Thorp I have put at the back of the book a list of earlier volumes and the titles of the poems taken from them. Somewhat more than half of the present collection appeared as *Selected Poems* in New York in 1937.

A. T.

CONTENTS

I

VIII

POEMS 1920-1945

SEASONS OF THE SOUL

To the memory of John Peale Bishop, 1892-1944

Allor porsi la mano un poco avante,
e colsi un ramicel da un gran pruno;
e il tronco suo gridò : Perchè mi schiante?

I. SUMMER

Summer, this is our flesh,
The body you let mature;
If now while the body is fresh
You take it, shall we give
The heart, lest heart endure
The mind's tattering
Blow of greedy claws?
Shall mind itself still live
If like a hunting king
It falls to the lion's jaws?

Under the summer's blast
The soul cannot endure
Unless by sleight or fast
It seize or deny its day
To make the eye secure.
Brothers in arms, remember
The hot wind dries and draws
With circular delay
The flesh, ash from the ember,
Into the summer's jaws.

It was a gentle sun
When, at the June solstice
Green France was overrun
With caterpillar feet.

No head knows where its rest is
Or may lie down with reason
When war's usurping claws
Shall take the heart escheat—
Green field in burning season
To stain the weevil's jaws.

The southern summer dies
Evenly in the fall:
We raise our tired eyes
Into a sky of glass,
Blue, empty, and tall
Without tail or head
Where burn the equal laws
For Balaam and his ass
Above the invalid dead,
Who cannot lift their jaws.

When was it that the summer
(Daylong a liquid light)
And the child, a new-comer,
Bathed in the same green spray,
Could neither guess the night?
The summer had no reason;
Then, like a primal cause
It had its timeless day
Before it kept the season
Of time's engaging jaws.

Two men of our summer world
Descended winding hell
And when their shadows curled
They fearfully confounded
The vast concluding shell:
Stopping, they saw in the narrow
Light a centaur pause
And gaze, then his astounded
Beard, with a notched arrow,
Part back upon his jaws.

It had an autumn smell
And that was how I knew
That I was down a well:
I was no longer young;
My lips were numb and blue,
The air was like fine sand
In a butcher's stall
Or pumice on the tongue:
And when I raised my hand
I stood in the empty hall.

The round ceiling was high
And the gray light like shale
Thin, crumbling, and dry:
No rug on the bare floor
Nor any carved detail
To which the eye could glide;
I counted along the wall
Door after closed door
Through which a shade might slide
To the cold and empty hall.

I will leave this house, I said,
There is the autumn weather—
Here, nor living nor dead;
The lights burn in the town
Where men fear together.
Then on the bare floor,
But tiptoe lest I fall,
I walked years down
Towards the front door
At the end of the empty hall.

The door was false—no key
Or lock, and I was caught
In the house; yet I could see
I had been born to it
For miles of running brought

Me back where I began.
I saw now in the wall
A door open a slit
And a fat grizzled man
Come out into the hall:

As in a moonlit street
Men meeting are too shy
To check their hurried feet
But raise their eyes and squint
As through a needle's eye
Into the faceless gloom,—
My father in a gray shawl
Gave me an unseeing glint
And entered another room!
I stood in the empty hall

And watched them come and go
From one room to another,
Old men, old women—slow,
Familiar; girls, boys;
I saw my downcast mother
Clad in her street-clothes,
Her blue eyes long and small,
Who had no look or voice
For him whose vision froze
Him in the empty hall.

III. WINTER

Goddess, sea-born and bright,
Return into the sea
Where eddying twilight
Gathers upon your people—
Cold goddess, hear our plea!
Leave the burnt earth, Venus,
For the drying God above,
Hanged in his windy steeple,
No longer bears for us
The living wound of love.

4

All the sea-gods are dead.
You, Venus, come home
To your salt maidenhead,
The tossed anonymous sea
Under shuddering foam—
Shade for lovers, where
A shark swift as your dove
Shall pace our company
All night to nudge and tear
The livid wound of love.

And now the winter sea:
Within her hollow rind
What sleek facility
Of sea-conceited scop
To plumb the nether mind!
Eternal winters blow
Shivering flakes, and shove
Bodies that wheel and drop—
Cold soot upon the snow,
Their livid wound of love.

Beyond the undertow
The gray sea-foliage
Transpires a phosphor glow
Into the circular miles:
In the centre of his cage
The pacing animal
Surveys the jungle cove
And slicks his slithering wiles
To turn the venereal awl
In the livid wound of love.

Beyond the undertow
The rigid madrepore
Resists the winter's flow—
Headless, unageing oak
That gives the leaf no more.
Wilfully as I stood
Within the thickest grove
I seized a branch, which broke;

I heard the speaking blood
(From the livid wound of love)

Drip down upon my toe:
"We are the men who died
Of self-inflicted woe,
Lovers whose stratagem
Led to their suicide."
I touched my sanguine hair
And felt it drip above
Their brother who, like them,
Was maimed and did not bear
The living wound of love.

IV. SPRING

Irritable spring, infuse
Into the burning breast
Your combustible juice
That as a liquid soul
Shall be the body's guest
Who lights, but cannot stay
To comfort this unease
Which, like a dying coal,
Hastens the cooler day
Of the mother of silences.

Back in my native prime
I saw the orient corn
All space but no time,
Reaching for the sun
Of the land where I was born:
It was a pleasant land
Where even death could please
Us with an ancient pun—
All dying for the hand
Of the mother of silences.

In time of bloody war
Who will know the time?
Is it a new spring star

Within the timing chill,
Talking, or just a mime,
That rises in the blood—
Thin Jack-and-Jilling seas
Without human will?
Its light is at the flood,
Mother of silences!

It burns us each alone
Whose burning arrogance
Burns up the rolling stone,
This earth—Platonic cave
Of vertiginous chance!
Come, tired Sisyphus,
Cover the cave's egress
Where light reveals the slave,
Who rests when sleeps with us
The mother of silences.

Come, old woman, save
Your sons who have gone down
Into the burning cave:
Come, mother, and lean
At the window with your son
And gaze through its light frame
These fifteen centuries
Upon the shirking scene
Where men, blind, go lame:
Then, mother of silences,

Speak, that we may hear;
Listen, while we confess
That we conceal our fear;
Regard us, while the eye
Discerns by sight or guess
Whether, as sheep foregather
Upon their crooked knees,
We have begun to die;
Whether your kindness, mother,
Is mother of silences.

II

THE MEDITERRANEAN

Quem das finem, rex magne, dolorum?

Where we went in the boat was a long bay
A slingshot wide, walled in by towering stone—
Peaked margin of antiquity's delay,
And we went there out of time's monotone:

Where we went in the black hull no light moved
But a gull white-winged along the feckless wave,
The breeze, unseen but fierce as a body loved,
That boat drove onward like a willing slave:

Where we went in the small ship the seaweed
Parted and gave to us the murmuring shore,
And we made feast and in our secret need
Devoured the very plates Aeneas bore:

Where derelict you see through the low twilight
The green coast that you, thunder-tossed, would win,
Drop sail, and hastening to drink all night
Eat dish and bowl to take that sweet land in!

Where we feasted and caroused on the sandless
Pebbles, affecting our day of piracy,
What prophecy of eaten plates could landless
Wanderers fulfil by the ancient sea?

We for that time might taste the famous age
Eternal here yet hidden from our eyes
When lust of power undid its stuffless rage;
They, in a wineskin, bore earth's paradise.

8

Let us lie down once more by the breathing side
Of Ocean, where our live forefathers sleep
As if the Known Sea still were a month wide—
Atlantis howls but is no longer steep!

What country shall we conquer, what fair land
Unman our conquest and locate our blood?
We've cracked the hemispheres with careless hand!
Now, from the Gates of Hercules we flood

Westward, westward till the barbarous brine
Whelms us to the tired land where tasseling corn,
Fat beans, grapes sweeter than muscadine
Rot on the vine: in that land were we born.

AENEAS AT WASHINGTON

I myself saw furious with blood
Neoptolemus, at his side the black Atridae,
Hecuba and the hundred daughters, Priam
Cut down, his filth drenching the holy fires.
In that extremity I bore me well,
A true gentleman, valorous in arms,
Disinterested and honourable. Then fled:
That was a time when civilization
Run by the few fell to the many, and
Crashed to the shout of men, the clang of arms:
Cold victualing I seized, I hoisted up
The old man my father upon my back,
In the smoke made by sea for a new world
Saving little—a mind imperishable
If time is, a love of past things tenuous
As the hesitation of receding love.

(To the reduction of uncitied littorals
We brought chiefly the vigour of prophecy,
Our hunger breeding calculation
And fixed triumphs)

                  The thirsty dove I saw
In the glowing fields of Troy, hemp ripening
And tawny corn, the thickening Blue Grass
All lying rich forever in the green sun.
I see all things apart, the towers that men
Contrive I too contrived long, long ago.
Now I demand little. The singular passion
Abides its object and consumes desire
In the circling shadow of its appetite.
There was a time when the young eyes were slow,
Their flame steady beyond the firstling fire,
I stood in the rain, far from home at nightfall
By the Potomac, the great Dome lit the water,
The city my blood had built I knew no more

While the screech-owl whistled his new delight
Consecutively dark.

                            Stuck in the wet mire
Four thousand leagues from the ninth buried city
I thought of Troy, what we had built her for.

TO THE ROMANTIC TRADITIONISTS

I have looked at them long,
My eyes blur; sourceless light
Keeps them forever young
Before our ageing sight.

You see them too—strict forms
Of will, the secret dignity
Of our dissolute storms;
They grow too bright to be.

What were they like? What mark
Can signify their charm?
They never saw the dark;
Rigid, they never knew alarm.

Do not the scene rehearse!
The perfect eyes enjoin
A contemptuous verse;
We speak the crabbed line.

Immaculate race! to yield
Us final knowledge set
In a cold frieze, a field
Of war but no blood let.

Are they quite willing,
Do they ask to pose,
Naked and simple, chilling
The very wind's nose?

They ask us how to live!
We answer: Again try
Being the drops we sieve.
What death it is to die!

Therefore because they nod,
Being too full of us,
I look at the turned sod
Where it is perilous

And yawning all the same
As if we knew them not
And history had no name—
No need to name the spot!

THE ANCESTORS

When the night's coming and the last light falls
A weak child among lost shadows on the floor,
It is your listening: pulse heeds the strain
Of fore and after, wind shivers the door.
What masterful delay commands the blood
Breaking its access to the living heart?
Consider this, the secret indecision,
Not rudeness of time but the systaltic flood
Of ancient failure begging its new start:
The flickered pause between the day and night
(When the heart knows its informality)
The bones hear but the eyes will never see—
Punctilious abyss, the yawn of space
Come once a day to suffocate the sight.
There is no man on earth who can be free
Of this, the eldest in the latest crime.

TO THE LACEDEMONIANS

*An old soldier on the night before the veterans' reunion talks partly
to himself, partly to imaginary comrades:*

The people—people of my kind, my own
People but strange with a white light
In the face: and the streets hard with motion
And the hard eyes that look one way.
Listen! the high whining tone
Of the motors, I hear the dull commotion:
I am come, a child in an old play.

I am here with a secret in the night;
Because I am here the dead wear gray.

It is a privilege to be dead; for you
Cannot know what absence is nor seize
The odour of pure distance until
From you, slowly dying in the head,
All sights and sounds of the moment, all
The life of sweet intimacy shall fall
Like a swift at dusk.

       Sheer time! Stroke of the heart
Towards retirement. . . .

        Gentlemen, my secret is
Damnation: where have they, the citizens, all
Come from? They were not born in my father's
House, nor in their fathers': on a street corner
By motion sired, not born; by rest dismayed.
The tempest will unwind—the hurricane
Consider, knowing its end, the headlong pace?
I have watched it and endured it, I have delayed
Judgment: it warn't in my time, by God, so
That the mere breed absorbed the generation!

Yet I, hollow head, do see but little;
Old man: no memory: aimless distractions.

I was a boy, I never knew cessation
Of the bright course of blood along the vein;
Moved, an old dog by me, to field and stream
In the speaking ease of the fall rain;
When I was a boy the light on the hills
Was there because I could see it, not because
Some special gift of God had put it there.
Men expect too much, do too little,
Put the contraption before the accomplishment,
Lack skill of the interior mind
To fashion dignity with shapes of air.
Luxury, yes—but not elegance!
Where have they come from?

              Go you tell them
That we their servants, well-trained, gray-coated
And haired (both foot and horse) or in
The grave, them obey . . . obey them,
What commands?

              My father said
That everything but kin was less than kind.
The young men like swine argue for a rind,
A flimsy shell to put their weakness in;
Will-less, ruled by what they cannot see;
Hunched like savages in a rotten tree
They wait for the thunder to speak: Union!
That joins their separate fear.

              I fought
But did not care; a leg shot off at Bethel,
Given up for dead; but knew neither shell-shock
Nor any self-indulgence. Well may war be
Terrible to those who have nothing to gain
For the illumination of the sense:
When the peace is a trade route, figures
For the budget, reduction of population,
Life grown sullen and immense
Lusts after immunity to pain.

There is no civilization without death;
There is now the wind for breath.

Waken, lords and ladies gay, we cried,
And marched to Cedar Run and Malvern Hill,
Kinsmen and friends from Texas to the Tide—
Vain chivalry of the personal will!

Waken, we shouted, lords and ladies gay,
We go to win the precincts of the light,
Unshadowing restriction of our day. . . .
Regard now, in the seventy years of night,

Them, the young men who watch us from the curbs:
They hold the glaze of wonder in their stare—
Our crooked backs, hands fetid as old herbs,
The tallow eyes, wax face, the foreign hair!

Soldiers, march! we shall not fight again
The Yankees with our guns well-aimed and rammed—
All are born Yankees of the race of men
And this, too, now the country of the damned:

Poor bodies crowding round us! The white face
Eyeless with eyesight only, the modern power—
Huddled sublimities of time and space,
They are the echoes of a raging tower

That reared its moment upon a gone land,
Pouring a long cold wrath into the mind—
Damned souls, running the way of sand
Into the destination of the wind!

MESSAGE FROM ABROAD

Paris, November 1929

*Their faces are bony and sharp but very red, although their
ancestors nearly two hundred years have dwelt by the miasmal
banks of tidewaters where malarial fever makes men gaunt and
dosing with quinine shakes them as with a palsy.*

"*Traveller to America*" (1799).

I

What years of the other times, what centuries
Broken, divided up and claimed?   A few
Here and there to the taste, in vigilance
Ceaseless, but now a little stale, to keep us
Fearless, not worried as the hare scurrying
Without memory . . .

                              Provence,
The Renascence, the age of Pericles, each
A broad, rich-carpeted stair to pride
With manhood now the cost—they're easy to follow
For the ways taken are all notorious,
Lettered, sculptured, and rhymed;
Those others, incuriously complete, lost,
Not by poetry and statues timed,
Shattered by sunlight and the impartial sleet.
What years. . . . What centuries. . . .

                              Now only
The bent eaves and the windows cracked,
The thin grass picked by the wind,
Heaved by the mole; the hollow pine that
Screams in the latest storm—these,
These emblems of twilight have we seen at length,

And the man red-faced and tall seen, leaning
In the day of his strength
Not as a pine, but the stiff form
Against the west pillar,
Hearing the ox-cart in the street—
His shadow gliding, a long nigger
Gliding at his feet.

II

Wanderers to the east, wanderers west:
I followed the cold northern track,
The sleet sprinkled the sea;
The dim foam mounted
The night, the ship mounted
The depths of night—
How absolute the sea!

With dawn came the gull to the crest,
Stared at the spray, fell asleep
Over the picked bones, the white face
Of the leaning man drowned deep;

The red-faced man, ceased wandering,
Never came to the boulevards
Nor covertly spat in the sawdust
Sunk in his collar
Shuffling the cards;

The man with the red face, the stiff back,
I cannot see in the rainfall
Down Saint-Michel by the quays,
At the corner the wind speaking
Destiny, the four ways.

III

I cannot see you
The incorruptibles,
Yours was a secret fate,
The stiff-backed liars, the dupes:

The universal blue
Of heaven rots,
Your anger is out of date—
What did you say mornings?
Evenings, what?
The bent eaves
On the cracked house,
That ghost of a hound. . . .
The man red-faced and tall
Will cast no shadow
From the province of the drowned.

IDIOT

The idiot greens the meadow with his eyes,
The meadow creeps implacable and still;
A dog barks, the hammock swings, he lies.
One two three the cows bulge on the hill.

Motion that is not time erects snowdrifts
While sister's hand sieves waterfalls of lace.
With a palm fan closer than death he lifts
The Ozarks and tilted seas across his face.

In the long sunset where impatient sound
Strips niggers to a multiple of backs
Flies yield their heat, magnolias drench the ground
With Appomattox! The shadows lie in stacks.

The julep glass weaves echoes in Jim's kinks
While ashy Jim puts murmurs in the day:
Now in the idiot's heart a chamber stinks
Of dead asters, as the potter's field of May.

All evening the marsh is a slick pool
Where dream wild hares, witch hazel, pretty girls.
"Up from the important picnic of a fool
Those rotted asters!" Eddy on eddy swirls

The innocent mansion of a panther's heart!
It crumbles, tick-tick time drags it in
Till now his arteries lag and now they start
Reverence with the frigid gusts of sin.

The stillness pelts the eye, assaults the hair;
A beech sticks out a branch to warn the stars,
A lightening-bug jerks angles in the air,
Diving. "I am the captain of new wars!"

The dusk runs down the lane driven like hail;
Far off a precise whistle is escheat
To the dark; and then the towering weak and pale
Covers his eyes with memory like a sheet.

ODE TO THE CONFEDERATE DEAD

Row after row with strict impunity
The headstones yield their names to the element,
The wind whirrs without recollection;
In the riven troughs the splayed leaves
Pile up, of nature the casual sacrament
To the seasonal eternity of death;
Then driven by the fierce scrutiny
Of heaven to their election in the vast breath,
They sough the rumour of mortality.

Autumn is desolation in the plot
Of a thousand acres where these memories grow
From the inexhaustible bodies that are not
Dead, but feed the grass row after rich row.
Think of the autumns that have come and gone!—
Ambitious November with the humours of the year,
With a particular zeal for every slab,
Staining the uncomfortable angels that rot
On the slabs, a wing chipped here, an arm there:
The brute curiosity of an angel's stare
Turns you, like them, to stone,
Transforms the heaving air
Till plunged to a heavier world below
You shift your sea-space blindly
Heaving, turning like the blind crab.

    Dazed by the wind, only the wind
    The leaves flying, plunge

You know who have waited by the wall
The twilight certainty of an animal,
Those midnight restitutions of the blood
You know—the immitigable pines, the smoky frieze
Of the sky, the sudden call: you know the rage,
The cold pool left by the mounting flood,
Of muted Zeno and Parmenides.

You who have waited for the angry resolution
Of those desires that should be yours tomorrow,
You know the unimportant shrift of death
And praise the vision
And praise the arrogant circumstance
Of those who fall
Rank upon rank, hurried beyond decision—
Here by the sagging gate, stopped by the wall.

    Seeing, seeing only the leaves
    Flying, plunge and expire

Turn your eyes to the immoderate past,
Turn to the inscrutable infantry rising
Demons out of the earth—they will not last.
Stonewall, Stonewall, and the sunken fields of hemp,
Shiloh, Antietam, Malvern Hill, Bull Run.
Lost in that orient of the thick and fast
You will curse the setting sun.

    Cursing only the leaves crying
    Like an old man in a storm

You hear the shout, the crazy hemlocks point
With troubled fingers to the silence which
Smothers you, a mummy, in time.
                  The hound bitch
Toothless and dying, in a musty cellar
Hears the wind only.
            Now that the salt of their blood
Stiffens the saltier oblivion of the sea,
Seals the malignant purity of the flood,
What shall we who count our days and bow
Our heads with a commemorial woe
In the ribboned coats of grim felicity,
What shall we say of the bones, unclean,
Whose verdurous anonymity will grow?
The ragged arms, the ragged heads and eyes
Lost in these acres of the insane green?

The gray lean spiders come, they come and go;
In a tangle of willows without light
The singular screech-owl's tight
Invisible lyric seeds the mind
With the furious murmur of their chivalry.

    We shall say only the leaves
    Flying, plunge and expire

We shall say only the leaves whispering
In the improbable mist of nightfall
That flies on multiple wing:
Night is the beginning and the end
And in between the ends of distraction
Waits mute speculation, the patient curse
That stones the eyes, or like the jaguar leaps
For his own image in a jungle pool, his victim.

What shall we say who have knowledge
Carried to the heart?   Shall we take the act
To the grave?   Shall we, more hopeful, set up the grave
In the house?   The ravenous grave?

                                Leave now
The shut gate and the decomposing wall:
The gentle serpent, green in the mulberry bush,
Riots with his tongue through the hush—
Sentinel of the grave who counts us all!

WINTER MASK

To the Memory of W. B. Yeats

I

Towards nightfall when the wind
Tries the eaves and casements
(A winter wind of the mind
Long gathering its will)
I lay the mind's contents
Bare, as upon a table,
And ask, in a time of war,
Whether there is still
To a mind frivolously dull
Anything worth living for.

II

If I am meek and dull
And a poor sacrifice
Of perverse will to cull
The act from the attempt,
Just look into damned eyes
And give the returning glare;
For the damned like it, the more
Damnation is exempt
From what would save its heir
With a thing worth living for.

III

The poisoned rat in the wall
Cuts through the wall like a knife,
Then blind, drying, and small
And driven to cold water,
Dies of the water of life:
Both damned in eternal ice,
The traitor become the boor
Who had led his friend to slaughter,
Now bites his head—not nice,
The food that he lives for.

IV

I supposed two scenes of hell,
Two human bestiaries,
Might uncommonly well
Convey the doom I thought;
But lest the horror freeze
The gentler estimation
I go to the sylvan door
Where nature has been bought
In rational proration
As a thing worth living for.

V

Should the buyer have been beware?
It is an uneven trade
For man has wet his hair
Under the winter weather
With only fog for shade:
His mouth a bracketed hole
Picked by the crows that bore
Nature to their hanged brother,
Who rattles against the bole
The thing that he lived for.

VI

I asked the master Yeats
Whose great style could not tell
Why it is man hates
His own salvation,
Prefers the way to hell,
And finds his last safety
In the self-made curse that bore
Him towards damnation:
The drowned undrowned by the sea,
The sea worth living for.

JUBILO

To Arthur Mizener

Hit mus' be now de Kingdom comin'
And de year of Jubilo

Tail-spinning from the shelves of sky
See how it dips and tacks and tosses
To cast a beam in the mind's eye:
Who will count the gains and the losses
   On the Day of Jubilo?

Public accountant with double entry
Enter in red war's final cast
In the black column the pacing sentry,
Old women picking the hogs' mast
   For the Day of Jubilo

Lean to the crowded air and hear,
Eavesdropper, how it goes inside
Your own deaf and roaring ear:
Boys caress the machines they ride
   On the Day of Jubilo

After the dry and sticking tongue
After our incivility:
Who will inflate the poet's lung
Gone flat of this indignity
   Till the Day of Jubilo?

Scholar, no dog will have your day
For all your capital's run out,
Wry baby in wet disarray—
Scholar, prepare your meagre clout
   For the Day of Jubilo

27

Under the slip and slide of day
Think, at the end you'll never be
Trapped in a fox-hole of decay
Nor snip nor glide of history
   After the Day of Jubilo

All our jubilant eyes are raised,
Jubilo. Over the barbican
On the great Day pure and dazed,
Empty of heart the empty man
   Of the Day of Jubilo

Then for the Day of Jubilo
The patient bares his arm at dawn
To suck the blood's transfusing glow
And then when all the blood is gone
   (For the Day of Jubilo)

Salt serum stays his arteries
Sly tide threading the ribs of sand,
Till his lost being dries, and cries
For that unspeakable salt land
   Beyond the Day of Jubilo.

HORATIAN EPODE TO THE DUCHESS
OF MALFI

DUCHESS: *Who am I?*
BOSOLA: *Thou art a box of worm-seed, at best but a salvatory
of green mummy.*

The stage is about to be swept of corpses.
You have no more chance than an infusorian
Lodged in a hollow molar of an eohippus.
Come, now, no prattle of remergence with the ὄντως ὄν.

.   .   .   .

As (the form requires the myth)
A Greek girl stood once in the prytaneum
Of Carneades, hearing mouthings of Probability,
Then mindful of love dashed her brain on a megalith

So you, O nameless Duchess who die young,
Meet death somewhat lovingly
And I am filled with a pity of beholding skulls.
There was no pride like yours.

Now considerations of the void coming after
Not changed by the "strict gesture" of your death
Split the straight line of pessimism
Into two infinities.

It is moot whether there be divinities
As I finish this play by Webster:
The street-cars are still running however
And the katharsis fades in the warm water of a yawn.

RETRODUCTION TO AMERICAN HISTORY

Cats walk the floor at midnight; that enemy of fog,
The moon, wraps the bedpost in receding stillness; sleep
Collects all weary nothings and lugs away the towers,
The pinnacles of dust that feed the subway.

What stiff unhappy silence waits on sleep
Struts like an officer; tongues next-door bewitch
Themselves with divination; I like a melancholy oaf
Beg the nightly pillow with impossible loves.
And abnegation folds hands, crossed like the knees
Of the complacent tailor, stitches cloaks of mercy
To the backs of obsessions.

                                        Winter like spring no less
Tolerates the air; the wild pheasant meets innocently
The gun; night flouts illumination with meagre impudence.

In such serenity of equal fates, why has Narcissus
Urged the brook with questions?   Merged with the element
Speculation suffuses the meadow with drops to tickle
The cow's gullet; grasshoppers drink the rain.
Antiquity breached mortality with myths.

Narcissus is vocabulary.   Hermes decorates
A cornice on the Third National Bank.   Vocabulary
Becomes confusion, decoration a blight; the Parthenon
In Tennessee stucco, art for the sake of death.   Now
(The bedpost receding in stillness) you brush your teeth
"Hitting on all thirty-two"; scholarship pares
The nails of Catullus, sniffs his sheets, restores
His "passionate underwear"; morality disciplines the other
Person; every son-of-a-bitch is Christ, at least Rousseau;
Prospero serves humanity in steam-heated universities, three
Thousand dollars a year.   Simplicity, Flamineo, is obscene;
Sunlight topples indignant from the hill.

In every railroad station everywhere every lover
Waits for his train.   He cannot hear.   The smoke
Thickens.   Ticket in hand, he pumps his body
Toward lower six, for one more terse ineffable trip,
His very eyeballs fixed in disarticulation.   The berth
Is clean; no elephants, vultures, mice or spiders
Distract him from nonentity: his metaphors are dead.
Notescatque magis mortuus atque magis
Nec tenuens texens sublimis aranea telam. . . . .

More sanitation is enough, enough remains: dreams
Do not end—lucidities beyond the stint of thought.
For intellect is a mansion where waste is without drain;
A corpse is your bedfellow, your great-grandfather dines
With you this evening on a cavalry horse.   Intellect
Connives with heredity, creates fate as Euclid geometry
By definition:

       The sunlit bones in your house
       Are immortal in the titmouse,
       They trip the feet of grandma
       Like an afterthought each day.
       These unseen sunlit bones,
       They may be in the cat
       That startles them in grandma
       But look at this or that
       They meet you every way.

For Pelops' and Tantalus' successions were at once simpler,
If perplexed, and less subtle than you think.   Heredity
Proposes love, love exacts language, and we lack
Language.   When shall we speak again?   When shall
The sparrow dusting the gutter sing?   When shall
This drift with silence meet the sun?   When shall I wake?

CAUSERIE

*. . . party on the stage of the Earl Carroll Theatre on Feb. 23.
At this party Joyce Hawley, a chorus-girl, bathed in the nude in a
bathtub filled with alleged wine.*—"*New York Times.*"

What are the springs of sleep?   What is the motion
Of dust in the lane that has an end in falling?
Heroes, heroes, you auguries of passion,
Where are the heroes with sloops and telescopes
Who got out of bed at four to vex the dawn?
Men for their last quietus scanned the earth,
Alert on the utmost foothill of the mountains;
They were the men who climbed the topmost screen
Of the world, if sleep but lay beyond it,
Sworn to the portage of our confirmed sensations,
Seeking our image in the farthest hills.
Now bearing a useless testimony of strife
Gathered in a rumour of light, we know our end
A packet of worm-seed, a garden of spent tissues.

I've done no rape, arson, incest, no murder,
Yet cannot sleep.   The petty crimes of silence
(Wary pander to whom the truth's chief whore)
I have omitted; no fool can say my tongue
Reversed its fetish and made a cult of conscience.
This innermost disturbance is a babble,
It is a sign moved to my face as well
Where every tide of heart surges to speech
Until in that loquacity of visage
One speaks a countenance fitter for death than hell.
Always your features lean to one direction
And by that charted distance know your doom.
For death is "morality touched with emotion,"
The syllable and full measure of affirmation
Give life the innocent crutch of quiet fools.

Where is your house, in which room stands your bed?
What window discovers these insupportable dreams?

In a lean house spawned on baked limestone
Blood history is the murmur of grasshoppers
Eastward of the dawn. Have you a daughter,
Daughters are the seed of occupations,
Of asperities, such as wills, deeds, mortgages,
Duels, estates, statesmen, pioneers, embezzlers,
"Eminent Virginians," reminiscences, bastards,
The bar-sinister hushed, effaced by the porcelain tub.
A daughter is the fruit of occupations;
Let her not read history lest knowledge
Of her fathers instruct her to be a petty bawd.
Vittoria was herself, the contemporary strumpet
A plain bitch.
                For miracles are faint
And resurrection is our weakest clause of religion,
I have known men in my youth who foundered on
This point of doctrine: John Ransom, boasting hardy
Entelechies yet botched in the head, lacking grace;
Warren thirsty in Kentucky, his hair in the rain, asleep;
None so unbaptized as Edmund Wilson the unwearied,
That sly parody of the devil. They lacked doctrine;
They waited. I, who watched out the first crisis
With them, wait:
                For the incredible image. Now
I am told that Purusha sits no more in their eyes.

Year after year the blood of Christ will sleep
In the holy tree, the branches sagged without bloom;
Then the plant overflowing the stale vegetation
In May the creek swells with the anemone,
The Lord God wastes his substance towards the ocean.
In Christ we have lived, on the flood of Christ borne up,
Who now is a precipitate flood of silence,
We a drenched wreck off an imponderable shore:
A jagged cloud is our memory of shore
Whereon we figure hills below ultimate ranges.
You cannot plot the tendency of man,
Whither it leads is not mysterious
In the various grave; but whence the impulse
To lust for the apple of apples on Christ's tree,
To desire in the eye, to penetrate your sleep,
Perhaps to catch in unexpected leaves

33

The light incentive of your absolute suspicion?
Over the mountains, the last barrier, you'd spill
These relics of your sires in a pool of sleep,
The sun being drained.
                            We have learned to require
In the infirm concessions of memory
The privilege never to hear too much.
What is this conversation, now secular,
A speech not mine yet speaking for me in
The heaving jelly of my tribal air?
It rises in the throat, it climbs the tongue,
It perches there for secret tutelage
And gets it, of inscrutable instruction—
Which is a puzzle like crepuscular light
That has no visible source but fills the trees
With equal foliage, as if the upper leaf
No less than the under were only imminent shade.

Manhood like a lawyer with his formulas
Sesamès his youth for innocent acquittal.

The essential wreckage of your age is different,
The accident the same; the Annabella
Of proper incest, no longer incestuous:
In an age of abstract experience, fornication
Is self-expression, adjunct to Christian euphoria,
And whores become delinquents; delinquents, patients;
Patients, wards of society.   Whores, by that rule,
Are precious.

                           Was it for this that Lucius
Became the ass of Thessaly?   For this did Kyd
Unlock the lion of passion on the stage?
To litter a race of politic pimps?   To glut
The Capitol with the progeny of thieves—
Where now the antique courtesy of your myths
Goes in to sleep under a still shadow?

FRAGMENT OF A MEDITATION

Not yet the thirtieth year, the thirtieth
Station where time reverses his light heels
To run both ways, and makes of forward back;
Whose long coördinates are birth and death
And zero is the origin of breath:
Not yet the thirtieth year of gratitude,
Not yet suffering but a year's lack,
All thanks that mid-mortality is done,
That the new breath on the invisible track
Winds anciently into my father's blood.

In the beginning the irresponsible Verb
Connived with chaos whence I've seen it start
Riddles in the head for the nervous heart
To count its beat on: all beginnings run
Like water the easiest way or like birds
Fly on their cool imponderable flood.

Then suddenly the noon turns afternoon
And afternoon like an ill-written page
Will fade, until the very stain of light
Gathers up all the venom of the night—
The equilibrium of the thirtieth age.

The thirtieth, not yet the thirtieth year
Of wonders, revelations, whispers, signs;
The impartial dumb truths of sound and sight
Strict beyond speech, immune to common fear.
Already the wind whistles the revelations
Of the time, but I'll go back seventy years
And more to the great Administrations:
Yet six had gone and all the public men
Whom doctrine and an evil nature made
Were only errand boys beaten by the sun
While Henry Adams fuddled in the shade.

I've heard what they said, in the running tap
Drawing water, their watery words, clear
Like a sad harlot's uselessly lucid pap
(I've heard the lion of S Street get his cheer),
I understood it, the general syllable
In a private ear, lost. . . .
                                    For who can tell
What the goat calls to the heifer, or the hen
Even to the cock her love? At thirty years
The years of the Christ, one will perceive, know,
Report new verity with a certain pen.

In the decade from eighteen-fifty-one
Where was Calhoun whose bristled intellect
Sumner the refined one did not admire?
I am convinced 'twas Calhoun who divined
How the great western star's last race will run
Unbridled round our personal defect,
Grinding its ash with engines of its mind.
" Too Southern and too simple," his death's head
Uttered a *Dies Irae* that last day
When Senator Mason in a voice to stun
Read off his speech; then put Calhoun to bed.
They put him in his grave. Does the worm say
In the close senate of tempestuous clay
That his intellect makes too difficult
The grave, as his enemies our life?
It's quiet there, for the worm's one fault
Is not discourtesy (give worms their dues)
In case the guest hurried by mortal strife
Enter the house in muddy overshoes.

It was a time of tributes; let me pay
Tribute to a man grandfather knew well
(Or so 'twas said, but one can never tell),
A stocky man but slight, no symmetry
Of face and eye, yet a distinction
Of the poet against the world; he dreamed the soul
Of the wide world and prodigies to come;
Exemplar of dignity, a gentleman
Who raised the black flag of the nether mind;
Hated in life by all; in death praised;

36

I cannot yet begin to understand
Why we are proud that an ancestor knew
The crazy Poe, who was not of our kind—
Bats in the belfry that round and round flew
In vapours not quite wholesome for the mind.

After Calhoun the local tenements
Of nature, tempered to the exigencies
Of air and fire, blurred with the public sense,
Diffused, while the Black Republicans
Took a short memory to their hot desire,
And honour turned a common entity
Crying decisions from the evening news.
Yet in a year, at thirty, one shall see
The wisdom of history, how she takes
Each epoch by the neck and, growling, shakes
It like a rat while she faintly mews.

Perhaps at the age of thirty one shall see
In the wide world the prodigies to come:
The long-gestating Christ, the Agnulus
Of time, got in the belly of Abstraction
By Ambition, a bull of pious use.
O Pasiphaë! mother of god, lest nature,
Peritonitis or morning sickness stunt
The growth of god in an unwholesome juice,
Eat cannon and cornflakes, that the lamb,
Spaceless as snow, may spare the rational earth
(Weary of prodigies and the Holy Runt)
A second prodigious, two-legged birth.

The signs and portents screaming in the air,
The nativity in my thirtieth year
Will glow in the heavens, the myriad fireflies
At the holy hour hovering round the house
Will stream in the night like flaming hair,
And man will scurry with averted eyes
Crouching, peering, silent, a drunken mouse.
The orange groves will blossom, the shining Sierras
Kindle all night far as Los Angeles;
With a noise, threatening, of wandering bees
Coming, angry with the air of their carouse,

The lamb through the sandpaper gates of life
(Made rougher by the bull's intenser strife)
Will leap, while the wild-eyed Pasiphaë
By the inscrutable wrath of glory stung
Hears the Wise Men * come swiftly from the sea.
The bull smoothly rolls his powerful tongue.

* I originally thought of the Wise Men as Mr. Herbert Hoover, the late Otto H. Kahn (an American banker and philanthropist), and the late Gertrude Stein; but I decided that the occasion required even wiser persons than these; and when I couldn't find them, I gave it up, and brought the poem to an abrupt end.
A. T.

ECLOGUE OF THE LIBERAL AND THE POET

LIBERAL

In that place, shepherd, all the men are dead.

POET

Yes, look at the water grim and black
Where immense Europa rears her head,
Her face pinched and her breasts slack.

LIBERAL

I said, shepherd, all the men are dead.

POET

Shall I turn to the road that goes America?
Is that a place for men to be dead
Or living? If you don't mind being asked.

LIBERAL

Try it and see. It's a pretty good way
To skim three thousand miles in a day
And none of them America.

POET

But what about her face and the tasked
Wonders of her air and soil, her big belly
That Putnam writes about under the sun?

LIBERAL

I don't know Put, I don't know his Nelly—
I'd name her that if she'd name it fun
But you know she hasn't any name,
Nowhere you touch her she's the same.

POET

What, shepherd, are we talking about?

LIBERAL

You started it, shepherd.

POET

Shepherd, I didn't.

LIBERAL

You did; you saw the poetical face of Europe.

POET

You said it was no place for men to be.

LIBERAL

I meant seawater; you thought I meant hope.

POET

Hell, I reckon you think I am a dope.

LIBERAL

I didn't say that; I said there was no place.

POET

If not in a place, where are the People weeping?

LIBERAL

They creep weeping in the face, not place.

POET

Is it something with which we may cope—
The weeping, the creeping, the peepee-ing, the peep-
ing?

LIBERAL

Hanging is something which I will do with this rope.

POET

Alas, for us who peep, weeping.
Alas, for us you see but little hope.

LIBERAL

Alas, I didn't say that; you rhymed hope with rope.
I meant I was going to hang us both for creeping.

POET

Afterwards they could process us into soap;
Afterwards they would rhyme soap with hope.

BOTH

What a cheerful rhyme! Clean not mean!
Been not seen! Not tired—expired!
We must now decide about place.
We decide that place is the big weeping face
And the other abstract lace of the race.

LIBERAL

Shepherd, what are we talking about?

POET

Oh, why, shepherd, are we stalking about?

FALSE NIGHTMARE

"I give the yawp barbaric
Of piety and pelf
(Who now reads Herrick?)

"And contradict myself—
No matter, the verse is large.
My five-and-ten cent shelf

"The continent is: my targe
Bigger than Greece.   The shock
Of Me exceeds its marge—

"Myself the old cock
With wind and water wild
(Hell with the privy lock):

"I have no woman child;
Onan-Amurikee
My son, alone, beguiled

"By my complacency
In priggery to slay
My blind posterity. . . ."

—These words, at dawn of day
In the sleep-awakened mind,
I made Walt Whitman say:

Wherefore I and my kind
Wear meekly in the face
A pale honey dew rind

Of rotten-sweet grace;
Ungracefully doating
Great-aunts hanged in lace

We are: mildly gloating
Dog bones in a trunk
Saved in the attic. . . .

Floating

Hating king and monk,
The classes and the mass,
We chartered an old junk

(Like Jesus on his ass)
Unto the smutty corn
And smirking sassafras.

In bulled Europa's morn
We love our land because
All night we raped her—torn,

Blue grass and glade. Jackdaws,
Buzzards and crows the land
Love with prurient claws;

So may I cunning my hand
To clip the increment
From the land or quicksand;

For unto me God sent
To gloze with iron bonds
The dozing continent—

The fallow graves, ponds
Full of limp fish, tall
Terrains, fields and fronds
Through which we crawl, and call.

THE TWELVE

There by some wrinkled stones round a leafless tree
With beards askew, their eyes dull and wild
Twelve ragged men, the council of charity
Wandering the face of the earth a fatherless child,
Kneel, at their infidelity aghast,
For where was it, somewhere in Syria
Or Palestine when the streams went red,
The victor of Rome, his arms outspread,
His eyes cold with that inhuman ecstasy,
Cried the last word, the accursèd last
Of the forsaken that seared the western heart
With the fire of the wind, the thick and the fast
Whirl of the damned in the heavenly storm:
Now the wind's empty and the twelve living dead
Look round them for that promontory Form
Whose mercy flashed from the sheet lightning's head;
But the twelve lie in the sand by the dry rock
Seeing nothing—the sand, the tree, rocks
Without number—and turn away the face
To the mind's briefer and more desert place.

SONNETS AT CHRISTMAS

(1934)

I

This is the day His hour of life draws near,
Let me get ready from head to foot for it
Most handily with eyes to pick the year
For small feed to reward a feathered wit.
Some men would see it an epiphany
At ease, at food and drink, others at chase
Yet I, stung lassitude, with ecstasy
Unspent argue the season's difficult case
So: Man, dull critter of enormous head,
What would he look at in the coiling sky?
But I must kneel again unto the Dead
While Christmas bells of paper white and red,
Figured with boys and girls spilt from a sled,
Ring out the silence I am nourished by.

II

Ah, Christ, I love you rings to the wild sky
And I must think a little of the past:
When I was ten I told a stinking lie
That got a black boy whipped; but now at last
The going years, with an accurate glow,
Reverse like balls englished upon green baize—
Let them return, let the round trumpets blow
The ancient crackle of the Christ's deep gaze.
Deafened and blind, with senses yet unfound,
Am I, untutored to the after-wit
Of knowledge, knowing a nightmare has no sound;
Therefore with idle hands and head I sit
In late December before the fire's daze
Punished by crimes of which I would be quit.

45

MORE SONNETS AT CHRISTMAS
(1942)

To Denis Devlin

I

Again the native hour lets down the locks
Uncombed and black, but gray the bobbing beard;
Ten years ago His eyes, fierce shuttlecocks,
Pierced the close net of what I failed: I feared
The belly-cold, the grave clout, that betrayed
Me slithering in the rift of cordial seas;
Ten years is time enough to be dismayed
By mummy Christ, head crammed between his knees.

Suppose I take an arrogant bomber, stroke
By stroke, up to the frazzled sun to hear
Sun-ghostlings whisper: Yes, the capital yoke—
Remove it and there's not a ghost to fear
This crucial day, whose decapitate joke
Languidly winds into the inner ear.

II

The day's at end and there's nowhere to go,
Draw to the fire, even this fire is dying;
Get up and once again politely lying
Invite the ladies toward the mistletoe
With greedy eyes that stare like an old crow.
How pleasantly the holly wreaths did hang
And how stuffed Santa did his reindeer clang
Above the golden oaken mantel, years ago!

Then hang this picture for a calendar,
As sheep for goat, and pray most fixedly
For the cold martial progress of your star,
With thoughts of commerce and society,
Well-milked Chinese, Negroes who cannot sing,
The Huns gelded and feeding in a ring.

III

Give me this day a faith not personal
As follows: The American people fully armed
With assurance policies, righteous and harmed,
Battle the world of which they're not at all.
That lying boy of ten who stood in the hall,
His hat in hand (thus by his father charmed:
"You may be President"), was not alarmed
Nor even left uneasy by his fall.

Nobody said that he could be a plumber,
Carpenter, clerk, bus-driver, bombardier;
Let little boys go into violent slumber,
Aegean squall and squalor where their fear
Is of an enemy in remote oceans
Unstalked by Christ: these are the better notions.

IV

Citizen, myself, or personal friend,
Your ghosts are Plato's Christians in the cave.
Unfix your necks, turn to the door; the nave
Gives back the cheated and light dividend
So long sequestered; now, new-rich, you'll spend
Flesh for reality inside a stone
Whose light obstruction, like a gossamer bone,
Dead or still living, will not break or bend.

Thus light, your flesh made pale and sinister
And put off like a dog that's had his day,
You will be Plato's kept philosopher,
Albino man bleached from the mortal clay,
Mild-mannered, gifted in your master's ease
While the sun squats upon the waveless seas.

ODE TO OUR YOUNG PRO-CONSULS
OF THE AIR

To St.-John Perse

Once more the country calls
From sleep, as from his doom,
    Each citizen to take
    His modest stake
Where the sky falls
With a Pacific boom.

Warm winds in even climes
Push southward angry bees
    As we, with tank and plane,
    Wrest land and main
From yellow mimes,
The puny Japanese.

Boys hide in lunging cubes
Crouching to explode,
    Beyond Atlantic skies,
    With cheerful cries
Their barking tubes
Upon the German toad.

Marvelling day by day
Upon the human kind
    What might I have done
    (A poet alone)
To baulk or slay
These enemies of mind?

I sought by night to foal
Chimeras into men—
    Decadence of power
    That, at late hour,
Untimed the soul
To live the past again:

Toy sword, three-cornered hat
At York and Lexington—
    While *Bon-Homme* whipped at sea
    This enemy
Whose roar went flat
After George made him run;

Toy rifle, leather hat
Above the boyish beard—
    And in that Blue renown
    The Gray went down,
Down like a rat,
And even the rats cheered.

In a much later age
(Europe had been in flames)
    Proud Wilson yielded ground
    To franc and pound,
Made pilgrimage
In the wake of Henry James.

Where Lou Quatorze held *fête*
For sixty thousand men,
    France took the German sword
    But later, bored,
Opened the gate
To Hitler—at Compiègne.

In this bad time no part
The poet took, nor chance:
    He studied Swift and Donne,
    Ignored the Hun,
While with faint heart
Proust caused the fall of France.

Sad day at Oahu
When the Jap beetle hit!
    Our Proustian retort
    Was Kimmel and Short,
Old women in blue,
And then the beetle bit.

49

It was defeat, or near it!
Yet all that feeble time
   Brave Brooks and lithe MacLeish
   Had sworn to thresh
Our flagging spirit
With literature made Prime!

Cow Creek and bright Bear Wallow,
Nursing the *blague* that dulls
   Spirits grown Eliotic,
   Now patriotic
Are: we follow
The *Irresponsibles!*

Young men, Americans!
You go to win the world
   With zeal pro-consular
   For our whole star—
You partisans
Of liberty unfurled!

O animal excellence,
Take pterodactyl flight
   Fire-winged into the air
   And find your lair
With cunning sense
On some Arabian bight

Or sleep your dreamless sleep
(Reptilian bomber!) by
   The Mediterranean
   And like a man
Swear you to keep
Faith with imperial eye:

Take off, O gentle youth,
And coasting India
   Scale crusty Everest
   Whose mythic crest
Resists your truth;
And spying far away

Upon the Tibetan plain
A limping caravan,
  Dive, and exterminate
  The Lama, late
Survival of old pain.
Go kill the dying swan.

ODE TO FEAR

Variation on a Theme by Collins

Let the day glare: O memory, your tread
Beats to the pulse of suffocating night—
Night peering from his dark but fire-lit head
Burns on the day his tense and secret light.

Now they dare not to gloss your savage dream,
O beast of the heart, those saints who cursed your name;
You are the current of the frozen stream,
Shadow invisible, ambushed and vigilant flame.

My eldest companion present in solitude,
Watch-dog of Thebes when the blind hero strove:
You, omniscient, at the cross-roads stood
When Laius, the slain dotard, drenched the grove.

Now to the eye of prophecy immune,
Fading and harried, you stalk us in the street
From the recesses of the August noon,
Alert world over, crouched on the air's feet.

You are our surety to immortal life,
God's hatred of the universal stain—
The heritage, O Fear, of ancient strife
Compounded with the tissue of the vein.

And I when all is said have seen your form
Most agile and most treacherous to the world
When, on a child's long day, a dry storm
Burst on the cedars, lit by the sun and hurled!

ELEGY

Jefferson Davis : 1808-1889

No more the white refulgent streets,
Never the dry hollows of the mind
Shall he in fine courtesy walk
Again, for death is not unkind.

A civil war cast on his fame,
The four years' odium of strife
Unbodies his dust; love cannot warm
His tall corpuscles to this life.

What did we gain? What did we lose?
Be still; grief for the pious dead
Suspires from bosoms of kind souls
Lavender-wise, propped up in bed.

Our loss put six feet under ground
Is measured by the magnolia's root;
Our gain's the intellectual sound
Of death's feet round a weedy tomb.

In the back chambers of the State
(Just preterition for his crimes)
We curse him to our busy sky
Who's busy in a hell a hundred times

A day, though profitless his task,
Heedless what Belial may say—
He who wore out the perfect mask
Orestes fled in night and day.

THE TRAVELLER

To Archibald MacLeish

The afternoon with heavy hours
Lies vacant on the wanderer's sight
And sunset waits whose cloudy towers
Expect the legions of the night

Till sullen thunder from the cave
Of twilight with deliberate swell
Whispers the air his darkening slave
To loose the nether bolts of hell

To crush the battlements of cloud
The wall of light around the West
So that the swarming dark will crowd
The traveller upon his quest

And all the air with heavy hours
Sinks on the wanderer's dull sight
And the thick dark whose hidden towers
Menace his travel to the night

Rolls forward, backward hill to hill
Until the seeker knows not where
Beyond the shade of Peacher's Mill
In the burnt meadow, with colourless hair

The secret ones around a stone
Their lips withdrawn in meet surprise
Lie still, being naught but bone
With naught but space within their eyes

Until bewildered by the road
And half-forgetful of his quest
The wanderer with such a load
Of breathing, being too late a guest

Turns back, so near the secret stone,
Falls down breathless at last and blind,
And the dark shift within the bone
Brings him the end he could not find.

THE OATH

It was near evening, the room was cold
Half dark; Uncle Ben's brass bullet-mould
And powder-horn and Major Bogan's face
Above the fire in the half-light plainly said:
There's naught to kill but the animated dead.
Horn nor mould nor major follows the chase.
Being cold I urged Lytle to the fire
In the blank twilight with not much left untold
By two old friends when neither's a great liar.
We sat down evenly in the smoky chill.
There's precious little to say betwixt day and dark,
Perhaps a few words on the implacable will
Of time sailing like a magic barque
Or something as fine for the amenities,
Till the dusk seals the window, the fire grows bright,
And the wind saws the hill with a swarm of bees.
Now meditating a little on the firelight
We heard the darkness grapple with the night
And give an old man's valedictory wheeze
From his westward breast between his polar jaws;
Then Lytle asked: Who are the dead?
Who are the living and the dead?
And nothing more was said. . . .
So I, leaving Lytle to that dream,
Decided what it is in time that gnaws
The ageing fury of a mountain stream
When suddenly as an ignorant mind will do
I thought I heard the dark pounding its head
On a rock, crying: *Who are the dead?*
Then Lytle turned with an oath—By God it's true!

DITTY

The moon will run all consciences to cover,
Night is now the easy peer of day;
Little boys no longer sight the plover
Streaked in the sky, and cattle go
Warily out in search of misty hay.
Look at the blackbird, the pretty eager swallow,
The buzzard, and all the birds that sail
With the smooth essential flow
Of time through men, who fail.

For now the moon with friendless light carouses
On hill and housetop, street and marketplace,
Men will plunge, mile after mile of men,
To crush this lucent madness of the face,
Go home and put their heads upon the pillow,
Turn with whatever shift the darkness cleaves,
Tuck in their eyes, and cover
The flying dark with sleep like falling leaves.

THE WOLVES

There are wolves in the next room waiting
With heads bent low, thrust out, breathing
At nothing in the dark: between them and me
A white door patched with light from the hall
Where it seems never (so still is the house)
A man has walked from the front door to the stair.
It has all been forever. A beast claws the floor.
I have brooded on angels and archfiends
But no man has ever sat where the next room's
Crowded with wolves, and for the honour of man
I affirm that never have I before. Now while
I have looked for the evening star at a cold window
And whistled when Arcturus spilt his light,
I've heard the wolves scuffle, and said: So this
Is man; so—what better conclusion is there—
The day will not follow night, and the heart
Of man has a little dignity, but less patience
Than a wolf's, and a duller sense that cannot
Smell its own mortality. (This and other
Meditations will be suited to other times
After dog silence howls his epitaph.)
Now remember courage, go to the door,
Open it and see whether coiled on the bed
Or cringing by the wall, a savage beast
Maybe with golden hair, with deep eyes
Like a bearded spider on a sunlit floor
Will snarl—and man can never be alone.

THE SUBWAY

Dark accurate plunger down the successive knell
Of arch on arch, where ogives burst a red
Reverberance of hail upon the dead
Thunder like an exploding crucible!
Harshly articulate, musical steel shell
Of angry worship, hurled religiously
Upon your business of humility
Into the iron forestries of hell:

Till broken in the shift of quieter
Dense altitudes tangential of your steel,
I am become geometries, and glut
Expansions like a blind astronomer
Dazed, while the worldless heavens bulge and reel
In the cold revery of an idiot.

THE EAGLE

Say never the strong heart
In the consuming breath
Cries out unto the dark
The skinny death.

Look! whirring on the rind
Of aether the white eagle,
Shot out of the mind,
The windy apple, burning,

Hears no more, past compass
In his topless flight,
The apple wormed, blown up
By the shells of light;

So, faggot of the heart
On the cinder day—
The woman and the man!
David and Sybil say

The world has a season
Under the world's might:
Now the deep autumn
A black apple in the night.

Think not the world spins ever
(Only the world has a year)
It's only the gaunt fierce bird
Flies, merciless with fear

Lest the air hold him not,
Beats up the scaffold of space
Sick of the world's rot—
God's hideous face.

LAST DAYS OF ALICE

Alice grown lazy, mammoth but not fat,
Declines upon her lost and twilight age;
Above in the dozing leaves the grinning cat
Quivers forever with his abstract rage:

Whatever light swayed on the perilous gate
Forever sways, nor will the arching grass,
Caught when the world clattered, undulate
In the deep suspension of the looking-glass.

Bright Alice! always pondering to gloze
The spoiled cruelty she had meant to say
Gazes learnedly down her airy nose
At nothing, nothing thinking all the day.

Turned absent-minded by infinity
She cannot move unless her double move,
The All-Alice of the world's entity
Smashed in the anger of her hopeless love,

Love for herself who, as an earthly twain,
Pouted to join her two in a sweet one:
No more the second lips to kiss in vain
The first she broke, plunged through the glass alone—

Alone to the weight of impassivity,
Incest of spirit, theorem of desire,
Without will as chalky cliffs by the sea,
Empty as the bodiless flesh of fire:

All space, that heaven is a dayless night,
A nightless day driven by perfect lust
For vacancy, in which her bored eyesight
Stares at the drowsy cubes of human dust.

—We too back to the world shall never pass
Through the shattered door, a dumb shade-harried crowd
Being all infinite, function depth and mass
Without figure, a mathematical shroud

Hurled at the air—blessèd without sin!
O God of our flesh, return us to Your wrath,
Let us be evil could we enter in
Your grace, and falter on the stony path!

THE TROUT MAP

The Management Area of Cherokee
National Forest, interested in fish,
Has mapped Tellico and Bald Rivers
And North River, with the tributaries
Brookshire Branch and Sugar Cove Creek:
A fishy map for facile fishery

In Marvel's kind Ocean: drawn in two
Colours, blue and red—blue for the hue
Of Europe (Tennessee water is green),
Red lines by blue streams to warn
The fancy-fishmen from protected fish;
Black borders hold the Area in a cracked dish

While other blacks, the dots and dashes, wire
The fisher's will through classic laurel
Over boar tracks to creamy pot-holes lying
Under Bald falls that thump the shying
Trout: we flew Professor, the Hackles and Worms.
(Tom Bagley and I were dotted and dashed wills.)

Up Green Cove gap from Preacher Millsap's cabin
We walked a confident hour of victory,
Sloped to the west on a trail that led us
To Bald River where map and scene were one
In seen-identity.   Eight trout is the story
In three miles.   We came to a rock-bridge

On which the road went left around a hill,
The river, right, tumbled into a cove;
But the map dashed the road along the stream
And we dotted man's fishiest enthymeme
With jellied feet upon understanding love
Of what eyes see not, that nourishes the will:

We were fishers, weren't we? And tried to fish
The egoed belly's dry cartograph—
Which made the government fish lie down and laugh.
(Tommy and I listened, we heard them shake
Mountain and cove because the map was fake.)
After eighteen miles our feet were clownish,

Then darkness took us into wheezing straits
Where coarse Magellan idling with his fates
Ran with the gulls for map around the Horn,
Or wheresoever the mind with tidy scorn
Revisits the world upon a dry sunbeam.
Now mapless the mountains were a dream.

THE MEANING OF LIFE

A Monologue

Think about it at will: there is that
Which is the commentary; there's that other,
Which may be called the immaculate
Conception of its essence in itself.
It is necessary to distinguish the weights
Of the two methods lest the first smother
The second, the second be speechless (without the first).
I was saying this more briefly the other day
But one must be explicit as well as brief.
When I was a small boy I lived at home
For nine years in that part of old Kentucky
Where the mountains fringe the Blue Grass,
The old men shot at one another for luck;
It made me think I was like none of them.
At twelve I was determined to shoot only
For honour; at twenty not to shoot at all;
I know at thirty-three that one must shoot
As often as one gets the rare chance—
In killing there is more than commentary.
One's sense of the proper decoration alters
But there's a kind of lust feeds on itself
Unspoken to, unspeaking; subterranean
As a black river full of eyeless fish
Heavy with spawn; with a passion for time
Longer than the arteries of a cave.

THE MEANING OF DEATH

An After-Dinner Speech

I rise, gentlemen, it is the pleasant hour.
Darkness falls.   The night falls.

                             Time, fall no more.
Let that be life—time falls no more.   The threat
Of time we in our own courage have forsworn.
Let light fall, there shall be eternal light
And all the light shall on our heads be worn

Although at evening clouds infest the sky
Broken at base from which the lemon sun
Pours acid of winter on a useful view—
Four water-towers, two churches, and a river:
These are the sights I give in to at night
When the long covers loose the roving eye
To find the horror of the day a shape
Of life: we would have more than living sight.
Past delusions are seen as if it all
Were yesterday flooded with lemon light,
Vice and virtue, hard sacrifice and crime
In the cold vanity of time.

                             Tomorrow
The landscape will respond to jocund day,
Bright roofs will scintillate with hues of May
And Phœbus' car, his daily circuit run,
Brings me to the year when, my time begun,
I loitered in the backyard by the alley;
When I was a small boy living at home
The dark came on in summer at eight o'clock
For Little Lord Fauntleroy in a perfect frock
By the alley: mother took him by the ear
To teach of the mixed modes an ancient fear.

Forgive me if I am personal.

                                        Gentlemen, let's
Forget the past, its related errors, coarseness
Of parents, laxities, unrealities of principle.

Think of tomorrow. Make a firm postulate
Of simplicity in desire and act
Founded on the best hypotheses;
Desire to eat secretly, alone, lest
Ritual corrupt our charity,
Lest darkness fall and time fall
In a long night when learned arteries
Mounting the ice and sum of barbarous time
Shall yield, without essence, perfect accident.

We are the eyelids of defeated caves.

THE CROSS

There is a place that some men know,
I cannot see the whole of it
Nor how I came there.   Long ago
Flame burst out of a secret pit
Crushing the world with such a light
The day-sky fell to moonless black,
The kingly sun to hateful night
For those, once seeing, turning back:
For love so hates mortality
Which is the providence of life
She will not let it blessèd be
But curses it with mortal strife,
Until beside the blinding rood
Within that world-destroying pit
—Like young wolves that have tasted blood,
Of death, men taste no more of it.
So blind, in so severe a place
(All life before in the black grave)
The last alternatives they face
Of life, without the life to save,
Being from all salvation weaned—
A stag charged both at heel and head:
Who would come back is turned a fiend
Instructed by the fiery dead.

V

INSIDE AND OUTSIDE

I

Now twenty-four or maybe twenty-five
Was the woman's age, and her white brow was sleek;
Lips parted in surprise, the flawless cheek;
The long brown hair coiled sullenly alive;
Her hands, dropt in her lap, could not arrive
At the novel on the table, being weak;
Nor breath, expunger of the mortal streak
Of nature, its own tenement contrive;

For look you how her body stiffly lies
Just as she left it, unprepared to stay,
The posture waiting on the sleeping eyes,
While the body's life, deep as a foul well,
Instinctive as the wind, busy as May,
Burns out a secret passageway to hell.

II

There is not anything to say to those
Speechless, who have stood up white to the eye
All night—till day, harrying they came too close,
Quarries the perils that at midnight lie
Waiting for those who hope to mortify
With foolish daylight their most anxious fear,
A bloodless and white fear that she may die
In the hushed room, and leave them soundless here:

There is no word that death can find to say
Deeper than life, savager than their time.
When Gabriel's trumpet ends all life's delay,
Will crash the beams of firmamental woe:
Not nature will sustain the even crime
Of death, though death sustains all nature, so.

F   69

DEATH OF LITTLE BOYS

When little boys grown patient at last, weary,
Surrender their eyes immeasurably to the night,
The event will rage terrific as the sea;
Their bodies fill a crumbling room with light.

Then you will touch at the bedside, torn in two,
Gold curls now deftly intricate with gray
As the windowpane extends a fear to you
From one peeled aster drenched with the wind all day.

And over his chest the covers in an ultimate dream
Will mount to the teeth, ascend the eyes, press back
The locks—while round his sturdy belly gleam
The suspended breaths, white spars above the wreck:

Till all the guests, come in to look, turn down
Their palms, and delirium assails the cliff
Of Norway where you ponder, and your little town
Reels like a sailor drunk in a rotten skiff.

The bleak sunshine shrieks its chipped music then
Out to the milkweed amid the fields of wheat.
There is a calm for you where men and women
Unroll the chill precision of moving feet.

THE ANABASIS

In Mem. L. N. L.   Ob. MCMXXXII

Noble beyond degree
In a democracy:
Slight woman whose spent grace
Banishes their vision
To the thin trackless air,
Stop now upon the stair
As they have seen you do
Meridional and true,
And with nut-brown hair
Restore location
To them now blinded quite
By the grave's after-light,
For unless it be done
The slave heart all alone
Strives timelessly
To go where you are gone—
Whether to vaults of air,
Imponderable nowhere,
Or the reducing sea—
The regions that are fair
Beyond heart's mastery.
They try your form to see
(Its lineless agony)
In our philosophy
Which stops, as cold and bare
As headless hair,
As lifeless as your bones,
Obtuse as meadow stones:
Re-corporated be!
(They cry you in despair)
Lest we, a blind race,
Imitate mortality
For all our living's pace,

And drawn into the bliss
Of your dispersèd face
Should join, before our place,
Death's long anabasis.

MR. POPE

When Alexander Pope strolled in the city
Strict was the glint of pearl and gold sedans.
Ladies leaned out more out of fear than pity
For Pope's tight back was rather a goat's than man's.

Often one thinks the urn should have more bones
Than skeletons provide for speedy dust,
The urn gets hollow, cobwebs brittle as stones
Weave to the funeral shell a frivolous rust.

And he who dribbled couplets like a snake
Coiled to a lithe precision in the sun
Is missing. The jar is empty; you may break
It only to find that Mr. Pope is gone.

What requisitions of a verity
Prompted the wit and rage between his teeth
One cannot say. Around a crooked tree
A moral climbs whose name should be a wreath.

TO A ROMANTIC

(1924)

To Robert Penn Warren

You hold your eager head
Too high in the air, you walk
As if the sleepy dead
Had never fallen to drowse
From the sublimest talk
Of many a vehement house.
Your head so turned turns eyes
Into the vagrant West;
Fixing an iron mood
In an Ozymandias' breast
And because your clamorous blood
Beats an impermanent rest
You think the dead arise
Westward and fabulous:
The dead are those whose lies
Were doors to a narrow house.

PROCESSION

Along the street with deliberative pomp
March the stiff minions of an ancient lord—
And have marched since fell the first shaken leaf
Into the withering hand of Ermengarde:
Crushing the silly meadow-sweet the hearse
Collects at every house the fragment curse.

The men on the hearse are deaf, every spring
They hear neither cry nor sweet civility;
Theirs is the margin between breath and breath,
Life's last, death's first; nor fore nor after see—
These must be wasting like shadows, are as brief
As the silken smile that stilled Correggio.

Gateways to morning on the dusty road
Open with jaws incuriously set;
Weeping, we follow like the steady toad
Drunk with his reverence. The mountain cat
Wheezes the air upon each granite crest
Raised on the good life's burial in the West.

The laughter and the shouting of delight
Of children flexed into a summer noon,
Chatter of women striating the crisp dark
The crinkled light of an imprisoned moon,
Stop for this silence, hesitate until
One rumour straight comes huddling on another
Of death, and death, and death!

UNNATURAL LOVE

Landor, not that I doubt your word,
That you had strove with none
At seventy-five and had deferred
To nature and art alone;
It is rather that at thirty-two
From us I see them part
After they served, so sweetly, you—
Yet nature has no heart:
Brother and sister are estranged
By his ambitious lies
For he his sister Helen much deranged—
Outraged her, and put coppers on her eyes.

EPISTLE

To Edmund Wilson, a Syracusan domiciled at Rome
(1927)

But though you're out of the age's curse
Reborn and by the circulation
Of tenser blood filling your verse
Winged to the lone and secret station

Of the full heart, yet, Cephalus,
Time should be long, the labour short;
You toil more than the most of us
For the idiot king of a savage court.

Your speeding thought is not the mind.
The mind's a sick eagle taking flight
Slowly, deliberate and unkind,
Ignorant, contemptuous of the light.

Wherefore, O Attic-raced, be still,
Lest borne in the blind important cab
By clotted stream and expensive hill,
You suddenly like an eager crab

Turn, asking whence flies the East
Or whither the dazed escaping West—
O Cephalus, you city-priest
Urging crab-like the busy quest!

Once we had marvelled country-wise,
My friend. You know that light was brief.
Mile after mile the cities rise
Where brisk Adonis tied the sheaf.

THE PROGRESS OF ŒNIA

His olim, ut fama est, vitiis ad proelia ventum est, his Troiana vides funera principiis.—PROPERTIUS.

I. MADRIGALE

Seed in your heart, warm dust transmuted
Gold, blooms in flakes of radiance
Arched in your face whereon my days,
Brinks of silence, glance.

Dream-emptied by some shifting
Monna Bice, you I resume:
Continually suffer the habitual
Cobra of my slightest gloom!

Release the happy hounds that trace
New smiles from the scampering wood
Of winter laughters—new prints of light
And trace them to your face!

II. IN WINTERTIME

I would not give the winter for a rose.
For remembering gold meadows and the hummer
Sucking them, I think June a time of pillage.
Your mouth is more passionate than any summer.

They say the spring holds many grapes
And green promises of fruit in the summer.
Give me your lips, Œnia, and let winter seas
Lash the cliffs and snows bite the grape.
We shall have passion without the sound of bees.

III. VIGIL

When you are dead and the frosty iron of laughter
Stupendously settles its pride upon your lips,
I will gather up the whispers you came after
When we first met, of immutable dissimulation.

If you are dead when the wind cries again
Over the bleak gables of an expected hour,
I will build a chapel out of the astonished pain
And wait for bells ringing in an empty tower.

IV. DIVAGATION

How many winds forget the sea!
Your dubious intention I forget
And look into the eager waste
Of your eyes careless of yesterday.

What cruel wine, what wayward gust
Tattering sun-hair to shreds of rain,
Swept you an exile to Cyrene
Blown by the swollen winds of pain,

I do not know, for we are dead:
Cluttering our youthful peace
With a various insolence, you laugh
The year, avid of love, to grief!

Our death, that was lonely, you've forgot;
Dawn came to us impatiently
Then went away with an equal fire,
Yet in an instant, in the rifted night,

This desolation is alive
With backward motions of bright feet—
Remembering the madness of scaling
A certain dusk to the first small star.

Whatever I have said to praise
Your wrath for me in better days
Than these, when the toughening grass
Fell tenderer for you to pass,
I say again, but differently—
As a still wind in a winter tree.
Pardon me! if turning over
In the reminiscence of a lover
The leaves of a desiccate romance,
I can but wonder if a chance
Invasion of a handsomer look
Than mine began you another book?
I shan't devise the same end
For other books—unless you send
Me word demanding back your hair.

Do you remember how your hair
Contained both ears? It never hid
Them quite, but climbed to a pyramid
More dazzling than superstitious kings
Set in the sand as their playthings;
And tell me, was it wantonness
Fluttering a diaphanous dress
That night at the Club when polite backs
Jazzed to the midnight cordax
And my veins raced to Seboim:
Not wantonness, but you were slim,
My dear, with a gift that I admired
For always being somehow tired!

Whatever else I say, your breast
Focused the witchery of the rest
Of a body vanished into a thought
If touched too late, or lately caught.
So more than your hair or olive eye
I remember your breast—does it still lie
Tactual billows in an upper world
Of superior sculpture, whence you hurled
Volcanic innocence and death
Out of the caverns beneath breath?

Œnia! forgive these sentiments
Of a respectful lover shattered in sense—
Yet sad that the modern bawd, grown dim,
Obscures the hotel cherubim
Whose red neckties had honoured this page
In a hotter, less barbaric age;
For now the languid stertorous
Pale verses of Propertius
And the sapphire corpse undressed by Donne
(Prefiguring Rimbaud's etymon)
Have shrunk to an apotheosis
Of cold daylight after the kiss.

And since helmets of steel bone rind
The great heads of the Numerous Mind
No glories of your breast and thighs
Shall these poor verses advertise—
Only the dry debility
Of a spent wind in a winter tree.

SHADOW AND SHADE

The shadow streamed into the wall—
The wall, break-shadow in the blast;
We lingered wordless while a tall
Shade enclouded the shadow's cast.

The torrent of the reaching shade
Broke shadow into all its parts,
What then had been of shadow made
Found exigence in fits and starts

Where nothing properly had name
Save that still element the air,
Burnt sea of universal frame
In which impounded now we were:

I took her hand, I shut her eyes
And all her shadow cleft with shade,
Shadow was crushed beyond disguise
But, being fear, was unafraid.

I asked fair shadow at my side:
What more shall fiery shade require?
We lay there in the immense tide
Of shade and shadowy desire

And saw the dusk assail the wall,
The black surge, mounting, crash the stone!
Companion of this lust, we fall,
I said, lest we should die alone.

PASTORAL

The enquiring fields, courtesies
And tribulations of the air—
Be still and give them peace:

The girl in the gold hair
With her young man in clover
In shadow of the day's glare

And there they were by the river
Where a leaf's light interval
Ringed the deep hurrying mirror;

Yet naught there to befall
Such meditations as beguile
Courage when love grows tall

For tall he was in green style
Of a willow shaking the pool.
"Let time be quiet as a mile,"

He said, "time is love's fool."
Yet time he would appease:
" Time, be easy and cool."

The enquiring courtesies
Of first dusk then debated
To cloud their agonies:

She, her head back, waited
Barbarous the stalking tide;
He, nor balked nor sated

But plunged into the wide
Area of mental ire,
Lay at her wandering side.

THE PARADIGM

For when they meet, the tensile air
Like fine steel strains under the weight
Of messages that both hearts bear—
Pure passion once, now purest hate;

Till the taut air like a cold hand
Clasped to cold hand and bone to bone
Seals them up in their icy land
(A few square feet) where into stone

The two hearts turning quickly pass
Once more their impenetrable world;
So fades out each heart's looking-glass
Whose image is the surface hurled

By all the air; air, glass is not;
So is their fleeting enmity
Like a hard mirror crashed by what
The quality of air must be.

For in the air all lovers meet
After they've hated out their love;
Love's but the echo of retreat
Caught by the sunbeam stretched above

Their frozen exile from the earth
And lost. Each is the other's crime.
This is their equity in birth—
Hate is its ignorant paradigm.

THE ROBBER BRIDEGROOM

Talk Between Bird and Girl

Turn back. Turn, young lady dear
A murderer's house you enter here

I was wooed and won little bird

(I have watched them come bright girls
Out of the rising sun, with curls)
The stair is tall the cellar deep
The wind coughs in the halls

I never wish to sleep

From the ceiling the sky falls
It will press you and press you, dear.

It is my desire to fear

(What a child! she desires her fear)
The house is whirling night, the guests
Grains of dust from the northwest

I do not come for rest

There is no rest for the dead

Ready for the couch of my groom

In a long room beneath the dew
Where the walls embrace and cling.

I wear my wedding ring

He will cut off your finger
And the blood will linger

Little bird!

MOTHER AND SON

Now all day long the man who is not dead
Hastens the dark with inattentive eyes,
The lady of the white hand and the erect head
Stares at the covers, leans for the son's replies
At last to her importunate womanhood—
That hand of death laid on the living bed;
Such is the fierce compositor of blood.

She waits; he lies upon the bed of sin
Where greed, avarice, anger writhed and slept
Till to their silence they were gathered in:
There, fallen with time, his tall and wicked kin
Once fired the passions that were never kept
In the permanent heart, and there his mother lay
To bear him on the impenetrable day.

The falcon mother cannot will her hand
Up to the bed, nor break the manacle
Her exile sets upon her harsh command
That he should say the time is beautiful—
Transfigured with her own devouring light:
The sick man craves the impalpable night.

Loosed betwixt eye and lid, the swimming beams
Of memory, that school of cuttlefish,
Rise to the air, plunge to the cold streams—
Rising and plunging the half-forgotten wish
To tear his heart out in a slow disgrace
And freeze the hue of terror to her face.

Hate, misery, and fear beat off his heart
To the dry fury of the woman's mind;
The son, prone in his autumn, moves apart
A seed blown upon a returning wind.
O child, be vigilant till towards the south

86

On the flowered wall all the sweet afternoon,
That reach of sun, swift as the cottonmouth,
Strikes at the black crucifix on her breast
Where the cold dusk comes suddenly to rest—
Mortality will speak the victor soon!

The dreary flies, lazy and casual,
Stick to the ceiling, buzz along the wall.
O heart, the spider shuffles from the mould
Weaving, between the pinks and grapes, his pall.
The bright wallpaper, imperishably old,
Uncurls and flutters, it will never fall.

A PAUPER

. . . and the children's teeth shall be set on edge.

I see him old, trapped in a burly house
Cold in the angry spitting of a rain
Come down these sixty years.

                              Why vehemently
Astride the threshold do I wait, marking
The ice softly pendent on his broken temple?
Upon the silence I cast the mesh of rancour
By which the gentler convergences of the flesh
Scatter untokened, mercilessly estopped.

Why so illegal these tears?

The years' incertitude and
The dirty white fates trickling
Blackly down the necessary years
Define no attitude to the present winter,
No mood to the cold matter.

(I remember my mother, my mother,
A stiff wind halted outside,
On the inner ear my country
Was a far shore crying
With invisible seas)

When tomorrow pleads the mortal decision
Sifting rankly out of time's sieve today,
No words differently will be uttered
Nor stuttered, like sheep astray.

A pauper in the swift denominating
Of a bald cliff with a proper name, having words
As strumpets only, I cannot beat off
Invincible modes of the sea, hearing:

Be a man my son by God.

                                He turned again
To the purring jet yellowing the murder story,
Deaf to the measured pathos of the air.

OBITUARY

In Memory of S. B. V., 1834-1909

. . . so what the lame four-poster gathered here
Between the lips of stale and seasoned sheets
Startles a memory sunlit upon the wall
(Motors and urchins contest the city streets)

While towards the bed the rigid shadows lean
Stung to the patience of all emptiness
And the bed empty where she kept,
Jerky gnats lunge at the haggard screen.

And now upstairs the lint that crusts the sills
Erodes in a windy shift along the floor.
Shall now her touselled eyes rinse out the haze
Of winter sprawled like a waif outside the door?

Feet answer: alternate and withdrawn
To the hard ease of lacquered pine that clamps
The shuffled fists into the breast and neck.

Time begins to elucidate her bones

Then you, so crazy and inviolate,
Will finger the console with a fearful touch,
Go past the horsehair sofa, the gilded frames
Whose faces are tired names
For the lifeblood that labours you so much.

CAPTAINS OF INDUSTRY

Captains of industry, your aimless power
Awakens harsh velleities of time:
Let you, brother, captaining your hour
Be zealous that your numbers are all prime,
Lest false division with sly mathematic
Plunder the inner mansion of the blood,
The Thracian, swollen with pride, besiege the Attic,
Invader foraging the sacred wood:
Yet the prime secret whose simplicity
Your towering engine hammers to reduce,
Though driven, holds that dyke against the sea
Which breached will turn unspeaking fury loose
To drown out him who swears to rectify
Infinity, that has nor ear nor eye.

EMBLEMS

I

Maryland, Virgina, Caroline
Pent images in sleep
Clay valleys rocky hills old fields of pine
Unspeakable and deep

Out of that source of time my farthest blood
Runs strangely to this day
Unkempt the fathers waste in solitude
Under the hills of clay

Far from their woe fled to its thither side
To a river in Tennessee
In an alien house I will stay
Yet find their breath to be
All that my stars betide—
There some time to abide
Took wife and child with me.

II

When it is all over and the blood
Runs out, do not bury this man
By the far river (where never stood
His fathers) flowing to the West,
But take him East where life began.
O my brothers, there is rest
In the depths of an eastward river
That I can understand; only
Do not think the truth we hold
I hold the slighter for this lonely
Reservation of the heart:
Men cannot live forever
But they must die forever

So take this body at sunset
To the great stream whose pulses start
In the blue hills, and let
These ashes drift from the Long Bridge
Where only a late gull breaks
That deep and populous grave.

III

By the great river the forefathers to beguile
Them, being inconceivably young, carved out
Deep hollows of memory on a river isle
Now lost—their murmur the ghost of a shout

In the hollows where the forefathers
Without beards, their faces bright and long,
Lay down at sunset by the cool river
In the tall willows, amid birdsong;

And the long sleep by the cool river
They've slept full and long, till now the air
Waits twilit for their echo; the burning shiver
Of August strikes like a hawk the crouching hare.

RECORDS

I. A DREAM

At nine years a sickly boy lay down
At bedtime on a cot by mother's bed
And as the two darks merged the room became
So strange it left that boy half dead:

The boy-man on the Ox Road walked along
The man he was to be and yet another,
It seemed the grandfather of his mother,
In knee-breeches silver-buckled like a song,
His hair long and a cocked hat on his head,
A straight back and slow dignity for stride;
The road, red clay sun-cracked and baked,
Led fearlessly through scrub pines on each side
Hour after hour—the old road cracked and burned,
The trees countless, and his thirst unslaked.
Yet steadily with discipline like fate
Without memory, too ancient to be learned,
The man walked on and as if it were yesterday
Came easily to a two-barred gate
And stopped, and peering over a little way
He saw a dog-run country store fallen-in,
Deserted, but he said, "Who's there?"
And then a tall fat man with stringy hair
And a manner that was innocent of sin,
His galluses greasy, his eyes coldly gray,
Appeared, and with a gravely learned air
Spoke from the deep coherence of hell—
The pines thundered, the sky blacked away,
The man in breeches, all knowledge in his stare,
A moment shuddered as the world fell.

II. A VISION

At twenty years the strong boy walked alone
Most fashionably dressed in the deserted park

94

At midnight, where the far lights burned low
And summer insects whined with little tone.
There was a final and comfortable dark
So that he walked deliberately slow;
It was not far from home, he'd been to see
His girl, who had sat silent and alone.
Picking his way upon the patched brick walk,
It being less dark near the street, he hastened
And knew a sense of fine immediacy
And then he heard some old forgotten talk
At a short distance like a hundred miles
Filling the air with its secrecy,
And was afraid of all the living air:
Now between steps with one heel lifted
A stern command froze him to the spot
And then a tall thin man with stringy hair,
Fear in his eyes, his breath quick and hot,
His arms lank and his neck a little twisted,
Spoke, and the trees sifted the air:
"I'm growing old," he said, "you have no choice,"
And said no more, but his bright eyes insisted
Incalculably with his relentless voice.

IGNIS FATUUS

In the twilight of my audacity
I saw you flee the world, the burnt highways
Of summer gave up their light: I
Followed you with the uncommon span
Of fear-supported and disbursèd eyes.

Towards the dark that harries the tracks
Of dawn I pursued you only. I fell
Companionless. The seething stacks
Of cornstalks, the rat-pillaged meadow
Censured the lunar interior of the night.

High in what hills, by what illuminations
Are you intelligible? Your fierce latinity
Beyond the nubian bulwark of the sea
Sustains the immaculate sight.

To the green tissue of the subterranean
Worm I have come back, two-handed from
The chase, and empty. I have pondered it
Carefully, and asked: Where is the light
When the pigeon moults his ease
Or exile utters the creed of memory?

VIII

THE VIGIL OF VENUS

(PERVIGILIUM VENERIS)

AN INTRODUCTORY NOTE

Few people today read the *Pervigilium Veneris*, and I doubt that it was ever widely read. Those of us who had some of the classical education which was still more or less compulsory in the colleges twenty-five years ago, did not read it in the Latin classes. Late Latin of the Decadence did not appear conspicuously in undergraduate "courses," the purpose of which was to hold up models of "purity" in the language and not to explore the range of the Latin sensibility in poetry. I came upon the poem I think in 1917, in the usual way, in *Marius the Epicurean*, where Pater gives us a somewhat overdone reconstruction of the circumstances of its origin. I looked up the Latin text and was disappointed. I was still too close to Swinburne in my adolescent revolt against his influence to read properly any poem about pagan love; I read the *Pervigilium* with Swinburne's sensibility, and heard it in his language, having then at any rate neither sensibility nor language of my own; and I disliked it. I did not look at the poem again until 1930, when I tried to work out a translation of the famous refrain. My attempt at this failed.

I go into this personal history in order to say what is obvious, that most verse is written accidentally, translations not excepted. In the fall of 1942 the refrain of the *Pervigilium* came back to me and for several days kept running through my head; then I suddenly knew that I "had" it. I had it, that is to say, in language that somewhat resembled English and in a metre that the English language can be written in: plain iambic pentametre, with anapaestic substitutions for the frequent falling rhythms of the original. The Latin is in trochaic septenarii, seven-footed lines with, at the end, an extra syllable which is usually accented, making eight accents: the metre, in fact, of Tennyson's *Locksley Hall*, which was actually used by some of the early translators of the *Pervigilium*. Except for certain special purposes it is an

97

impossible metre in English, for unless the extra accented syllable at the end is managed with great skill the line will break down into units of four and three and sound like a Wesleyan hymn— a high price to pay for metrical fidelity to a foreign original.

The poem is supposed by some scholars to have been written as early as the reign of Hadrian (A.D. 117-138) by a man named Florus, who was better known as historian and rhetorician than as poet. This conjecture is based upon the scholars' feeling that the poem ought to have been written then, since under Hadrian the *trinoctium* of Venus, the spring ritual of the cult of Dione, or Venus Genetrix, whom the poem celebrates as the principle of sexual reproduction in nature, was officially encouraged and even given the dignity of a state religion. But certain features of the poem might place it much later, as late, perhaps, as the fourth century. The late J. W. Mackail saw in it "a certain affinity of style and spirit" with the Eclogues of Nemesianus of Carthage (*cir.* A.D. 285), and an even more striking resemblance to the fragments of Tiberianus, another African poet, who wrote around A.D. 350. If I were entitled to an opinion I should side with Mackail, for although the simplified syntax and the stressed verse could have been written as early as Hadrian, it is not probable that they were: the language of the poem seems to stand midway between classical Latin and late vulgar Latin which toward the end of the empire began to show, in the levelling off of the inflectional system, the influence of the popular and provincial tongues. The reader of the *Pervigilium*, who has only a little Latin, as I have, will observe the occasional rhyme, the line unit of expression (rare in the poetry of the Golden Age), the frequent coincidence of quantity and stress, and even in some instances stress crowding out the quantities of the vowels.

The delicacy of feeling and the subtlety of the simple language require little demonstration. There is, of course, a good deal of merely conventional stuff, for which there is no equivalent convention in English; for example, the standard references to Venus as the founder of Rome. This material, brought into our language, had to be considerably doctored in the eighteenth-century manner to make it palatable at all. I have not found any scholar or previous translator who does justice to the restrained humour of the lines about Cupid and the virgins. Up to the last two stanzas the poem is moving, it has its peculiar subtleties; but it is not brilliant. In those two last stanzas something like a first-rate lyrical imagination suddenly appears.

Observe how it works. The "maid of Tereus" is the sort of classical parable that we have had throughout the poem; but here it is not a conventional allusion. The beautiful line:

iam loquaces ore rauco stagna cycni perstrepunt

particularizes the scene about to be presented as no other scene in the poem has been particularized: we feel immediately the presence of a dramatic observer, an ear that listens and an eye that sees. *Terei puella* is more than a classical allusion; she is a real bird singing in a real poplar tree, answering the dissonance of the swans as they strike the surface of the lake.

Is she Philomela or Procne, swallow or nightingale? Our anonymous poet is not explicit; yet in the next and last stanza he speaks of the swallow who has ceased to be silent and can now sing. We evidently have here the older Greek, not the later Latin, version of the story of the rape of Philomela, in which Procne becomes the nightingale, Philomela the swallow. (It is perhaps significant that the poet uses the Greek *chelidon* instead of the Latin *hirundo* for swallow.) Countless versions of the tale circulated in the ancient world. The brief summary by Apollodorus, who collected in the second century B.C. virtually all the known Greek myths in a long work that comes down to us as *The Library*, gives the story as it must have been most widely known among the Greeks:

> . . . and having with his help brought the war to a successful close he (Pandion) gave Tereus his own daughter Procne in marriage. Tereus had by her a son Itys, and having fallen in love with Philomela (sister to Procne), he seduced her also saying that Procne was dead, for he concealed her in the country. Afterward he married Philomela and bedded with her and cut out her tongue. But by weaving characters in a robe she revealed thereby to Procne her own sorrows. And having sought out her sister, Procne killed her son Itys, boiled him, and served him up for supper to the unwitting Tereus, and fled with her sister. . . . When Tereus was aware of what had happened, he snatched up an axe and pursued them. And being overtaken at Daulia in Phocis, they prayed the gods to be turned into birds, and Procne became a nightingale and Philomela a swallow.—(APOLLODORUS, *The Library*, III, xiv: Loeb Classical Library, pp. 99-100.)

The late Sir J. G. Frazer, editor of the Loeb text of Apollodorus, says in a note on this passage: "The later Roman mythographers somewhat absurdly inverted the transformation of the two sisters, making Procne the swallow and the tongueless Philomela the songstress nightingale." While I was translating the *Pervigilium* I assumed that our poet had followed Ovid's version of the transformation, but upon looking up the story in the *Metamorphoses* (VI, 424-675) I found that I had not remembered Ovid accurately, for he does not tell us what kind of birds the sisters became; he merely says:

> *corpora Cecropidum pennis pendere putares :*
> *pendebant pennis.*

Yet it must be confessed that the "internal evidence" in favour of the belief that the bird singing *subter umbram populi* is Philomela the swallow is not conclusive. If we translate *puella*, in the phrase *Terei puella*, in the rare sense of wife, the bird is Procne the nightingale; and we may only surmise that the poet, when he asks, *Quando fiam uti chelidon ut tacere desinam?* is hoping that he may become as the swallow companion to the nightingale. This interpretation has, I think, little to recommend it; but the reader may take his choice.

The symbolic power of the scene in stanza XXI is firmly grounded in the dramatic perception of the poet, whose personality has not previously appeared. It appears explicitly in stanza XXII, where this long, gentle meditation on the sources of all life comes to a climax in the poet's sudden consciousness of his own feeble powers. When shall I, he says, like Philomela the swallow, suffer violence and be moved to sing? It is this unexpected and dramatic ending that makes, for me, what were otherwise an interesting ritualistic chant, one of the finest of lyric poems. Perhaps in the Amyclae, the people of the town of that name in Latium who were called *tacitae*, and who, when menaced by an enemy, could not speak for help and were destroyed, we may see an image of all "late" people. I like to think that the *Amyclae tacitae* were not Latians but lived in the Laconian town of that name, where Apollo was the tutelary deity under the surname Amyclaeus, and that having offended their god, the Laconian Amyclae were cursed with silence and died of their own emptiness of song. May we see something of this in the last stanza of the poem? If there is any external evidence for it I have not been able to find it. Yet is the poem not telling us that the loss of symbolic language may mean the extinction of our humanity?

The text that I have followed is Mackail's, which was first published in 1888 and which now appears in the Loeb Classical Library. Mackail's arrangement of the corrupt text into quatrains is perhaps a triumph of textual scholarship. The poem comes down to us in two badly confused manuscripts in the *Anthologia Latina*, a miscellany of short poems of the Silver Age. In order to bring together material that seemed to go together, and to improve the continuity, I have shifted in several instances Mackail's order of the stanzas, a liberty that seemed justified by the corruption of the surviving texts; for no one knows the original order. Where I have moved a stanza I have indicated in brackets, in the Latin text, the number of the stanza in Mackail's arrangement. For the translation of the first line of stanza XXI I am indebted to my wife; and for constant criticism, to Robert Lowell. A. T.

MONTEAGLE, TENNESSEE.
April 27, 1943.

PERVIGILIUM VENERIS

I

Cras amet qui nunquam amavit quique amavit cras amet:
ver novum, ver iam canorum, ver renatus orbis est;
vere concordant amores, vere nubunt alites,
et nemus comam resolvit de maritis imbribus.

cras amet qui nunquam amavit quique amavit cras amet.

II (III)

cras erit cum primus aether copulavit nuptias:
tunc cruore de superno spumeo et ponti globo,
caerulas inter catervas, inter et bipedes equos,
fecit undantem Dionem de maritis imbribus.

cras amet qui nunquam amavit quique amavit cras amet.

III (II)

cras amorum copulatrix inter umbras arborum
implicat casas virentes de flagello myrteo:
cras canoris feriatos ducit in silvis choros;
cras Dione iura dicit fulta sublimi throno.

cras amet qui nunquam amavit quique amavit cras amet.

IV

ipsa gemmis purpurantem pingit annum floridis;
ipsa turgentes papillas de favoni spiritu
urget in nodos tepentes; ipsa roris lucidi,
noctis aura quem relinquit, spargit umentes aquas.

cras amet qui nunquam amavit quique amavit cras amet.

V

emicant lacrimae trementes de caduco pondere,
gutta praeceps orbe parvo sustinet casus suos:
umor ille quem serenis astra rorant noctibus
mane virgines papillas solvit umenti peplo.

cras amet qui nunquam amavit quique amavit cras amet.

THE VIGIL OF VENUS

I

Tomorrow let loveless, let lover tomorrow make love:
O spring, singing spring, spring of the world renew!
In spring lovers consent and the birds marry
When the grove receives in her hair the nuptial dew.

    Tomorrow may loveless, may lover tomorrow make love.

II

Tomorrow's the day when the prime Zeus made love:
Out of lightning foam shot deep in the heaving sea
(Witnessed by green crowds of finny horses)
Dione rising and falling, he made to be!

    Tomorrow may loveless, may lover tomorrow make love.

III

Tomorrow the Joiner of love in the gracious shade
Twines her green huts with boughs of myrtle claws,
Tomorrow leads her gangs to the singing woods:
Tomorrow Dione, on high, lays down the laws.

    Tomorrow may loveless, may lover tomorrow make love.

IV

She shines the tarnished year with glowing buds
That, wakening, head up to the western wind
In eager clusters. Goddess! You deign to scatter
Lucent night-drip of dew; for you are kind.

    Tomorrow may loveless, may lover tomorrow make love.

V

The heavy teardrops stretch, ready to fall,
Then falls each glistening bead to the earth beneath:
The moisture that the serene stars sent down
Loosens the virgin bud from the sliding sheath.

    Tomorrow may loveless, may lover tomorrow make love.

VI

en pudorem florulentæ prodiderunt purpuræ
et rosarum flamma nodis emicat tepentibus.
ipsa iussit diva vestem de papillis solvere,
ut recenti mane nudae virgines nubant rosae.

   cras amet qui nunquam amavit quique amavit cras amet.

VII

facta Cypridis de cruore deque Amoris osculo,
deque gemmis deque flammis deque solis purpuris,
cras ruborem qui latebat veste tectus ignea
uvido marita nodo non pudebit solvere.

   cras amet qui nunquam amavit quique amavit cras amet.

VIII

ipsa numphas diva luco iussit ire myrteo:
it puer comes puellis; nec tamen credi potest
esse Amorem feriatum, si sagittas vexerit:
ite nymphae, posuit arma, feriatus est Amor.

   cras amet qui nunquam amavit quique amavit cras amet.

IX

iussus est inermis ire, nudus ire iussus est,
neu quid arcu neu sagitta neu quid igne laederet
sed tamen cavete nymphae, quod Cupido pulcher est:
totus est inermis idem quando nudus est Amor.

   cras amet qui nunquam amavit quique amavit cras amet.

X (XIV)

ruris hic erunt puellae vel puellae montium
quaeque silvas quaeque lucos quaeque fontes incolunt:
iussit omnes adsidere mater alitis dei,
iussit et nudo puellas nil Amori credere.

   cras amet qui nunquam amavit quique amavit cras amet.

Look, the high crimsons have revealed their shame.
The burning rose turns in her secret bed,
The goddess has bidden the girdle to loose its folds
That the rose at dawn may give her maidenhead.

Tomorrow may loveless, may lover tomorrow make love.

VII

The blood of Venus enters her blood, Love's kiss
Has made the drowsy virgin modestly bold;
Tomorrow the bride is not ashamed to take
The burning taper from its hidden fold.

Tomorrow may loveless, may lover tomorrow make love.

VIII

The goddess herself has sent nymphs to the woods,
The Boy with girls to the myrtles; perhaps you think
That Love's not truly tame if he shows his arrows?
Go, girls! Unarmed, Love beckons. You must not shrink.

Tomorrow may loveless, may lover tomorrow make love.

IX

Bidden unarmed to go and to go naked
Lest he destroy with bow, with dart, with brand—
Yet, girls, Cupid is pretty, and you must know
That Love unarmed can pierce with naked hand!

Tomorrow may loveless, may lover tomorrow make love.

X

Here will be girls of the farm and girls of the mountain
And girls who live by forest, or grove, or spring.
The mother of the Flying Boy has smiled
And said: Now, girls, beware his naked sting!

Tomorrow may loveless, may lover tomorrow make love.

ipsa vellet te rogare, si pudicam flecteret;
ipsa vellet ut venires, si deceret virginem:
iam tribus choros videres feriatos noctibus
congreges inter catervas ire per saltus tuos.

cras amet qui nunquam amavit quique amavit cras amet.

XII (X)

conpari Venus pudore mittit ad te virgines:
una res est quam rogamus, cede virgo Delia,
ut nemus sit incruentum de ferinis stragibus
et recentibus virentes ducat umbras floribus.

cras amet qui nunquam amavit quique amavit cras amet.

XIII (XII)

floreas inter coronas, myrteas inter casas,
nec Ceres nec Bacchus absunt nec poetarum deus.
de tenente tota nox est perviglanda canticis:
regnet in silvis Dione, tu recede Delia.

cras amet qui nunquam amavit quique amavit cras amet.

XIV (XIII)

iussit Hyblaeis tribunal stare diva floribus;
praeses ipsa iura dicet, adsidebunt Gratiae:
Hybla totos funde flores, quicquid annus adtulit;
Hybla florum sume vestem, quantus Ennae campus est.

cras amet qui nunquam amavit quique amavit cras amet.

XV

ut pater totum crearet veris annum nubibus
in sinum maritus imber fluxit almae coniugis,
unde fetus perque pontum perque caelum pergeret
perque terras mixtus omnes alere magno corpore.

cras amet qui nunquam amavit quique amavit cras amet.

Gently she asks may she bend virginity?
Gently that you, a modest girl, may yield.
Now, should you come, for three nights you would see
Delirious bands in every grove and field.

Tomorrow may loveless, may lover tomorrow make love.

XII

Venus herself has maidens as pure as you;
So, Delia, one thing only we ask: Go away!
That the wood shall not be bloody with slaughtered beasts
When Venus flicks the shadows with greening spray.

Tomorrow may loveless, may lover tomorrow make love.

XIII

Among the garlands, among the myrtle bowers
Ceres and Bacchus, and the god of verse, delay.
Nightlong the watch must be kept with votive cry—
Dione's queen of the woods: Diana, make way!

Tomorrow may loveless, may lover tomorrow make love.

XIV

She places her court among the flowers of Hybla;
Presiding, she speaks her laws; the Graces are near.
Hybla, give all your blossoms, and bring, Hybla,
The brightest plain of Enna for the whole year.

Tomorrow may loveless, may lover tomorrow make love.

XV

With spring the father-sky remakes the world:
The male shower has flowed into the bride,
Earth's body; then shifted through sky and sea and land
To touch the quickening child in her deep side.

Tomorrow may loveless, may lover tomorrow make love.

XVI (XVII)

pervium sui tenorem seminali tramite
perque caelum perque terras perque pontum subditum
ipsa duxit, ipsa venis procreantem spiritum
inbuit, iussitque mundum nosse nascendi vias.

    cras amet qui nunquam amavit quique amavit cras amet.

XVII (XVI)

ipsa venas atque mentem permeanti spiritu
intus occultis gubernat procreatrix viribus.
ipsa Troianos nepotes in Latinos transtulit,
Romuleas ipsa fecit cum Sabinis nuptias.

    cras amet qui nunquam amavit quique amavit cras amet.

XVIII

ipsa Laurentem puellam coniugem nato dedit,
moxque Marti de sacello dat pudicam virginem,
unde Ramnes et Quirites proque prole posterum
Romulum patrem crearet et nepotem Caesarem.

    cras amet qui nunquam amavit quique amavit cras amet.

XIX

rura fecundat voluptas: rura Venerem sentiunt:
ipse Amor puer Dionae rure natus creditur:
hunc ager cum parturiret ipsa suscepit sinu,
ipsa florum delicatis educavit osculis.

    cras amet qui nunquam amavit quique amavit cras amet.

XX

ecce iam super genestas explicant tauri latus,
quisque coetus continetur coniugali foedere:
subter umbras cum maritis ecce balantum gregem,
et canoras non tacere diva iussit alites.

    cras amet qui nunquam amavit quique amavit cras amet.

XVI

Over sky and land and down under the sea
On the path of the seed the goddess brought to earth
And dropped into our veins created fire,
That men might know the mysteries of birth.

Tomorrow may loveless, may lover tomorrow make love.

XVII

Body and mind the inventive Creatress fills
With spirit blowing its invariable power:
The Sabine girls she gave to the sons of Rome
And sowed the seed exiled from the Trojan tower.

Tomorrow may loveless, may lover tomorrow make love.

XVIII

Lavinia of Laurentum she chose to bed
Her son Aeneas, and for the black Mars won
The virgin Silvia, to found the Roman line:
Sire Romulus and Caesar, her grandson.

Tomorrow may loveless, may lover tomorrow make love.

XIX

Venus knows country matters: country knows Venus:
For Love, Dione's boy, was born on the farm.
From the rich furrow she snatched him to her breast,
With tender flowers taught him peculiar charm.

Tomorrow may loveless, may lover tomorrow make love.

XX

See how the bullocks rub their flanks with broom!
See the ram pursue through the shade the bleating ewe,
For lovers' union is Venus in kind pursuit;
And she tells the birds to forget their winter woe.

Tomorrow may loveless, may lover tomorrow make love.

XXI

iam loquaces ore rauco stagna cycni perstrepunt:
adsonat Terei puella subter umbram populi,
ut potes motus amoris ore dici musicos,
et neges queri sororem de marito barbaro.

cras amet qui nunquam amavit quique amavit cras amet.

XXII

illa cantat, nos tacemus: quando ver venit meum?
quando fiam uti chelidon ut tacere desinam?
perdidi musam tacendo, nec me Apollo respicit:
sic Amyclas, cum tacerent, perdidit silentium.

cras amet qui nunquam amavit quique amavit cras amet.

XXI

Now the tall swans with hoarse cries thrash the lake:
The girl of Tereus pours from the poplar ring
Musical change—sad sister who bewails
Her act of darkness with the barbarous king!

   Tomorrow may loveless, may lover tomorrow make love.

XXII

She sings, we are silent. When will my spring come?
Shall I find my voice when I shall be as the swallow?
Silence destroyed the Amyclae: they were dumb.
Silent, I lost the muse. Return, Apollo!

   Tomorrow let loveless, let lover tomorrow make love.

BIBLIOGRAPHICAL NOTE

The poems collected here were first printed in four earlier volumes. The titles of the poems with the books from which they were taken are as follows:

Mr. Pope and Other Poems (1928)

Ode to the Confederate Dead
Death of Little Boys
Ditty
Epistle to Edmund Wilson
Horatian Epode to the Duchess of Malfi
Idiot
Inside and Outside
Mr. Pope
Obituary
The Progress of Œnia
A Pauper
Procession
Retroduction to American History
To a Romantic
The Subway
Ignis Fatuus

Poems: 1928-1931 (1932)

Causerie
The Cross
Records
The Eagle
Elegy
Emblems
Ode to Fear
Inside and Outside
Last Days of Alice
Message from Abroad
Mother and Son
The Oath
The Paradigm
The Traveller
The Twelve
The Wolves
Captains of Industry (Sonnet IX, from Sonnets of the Blood)

The Mediterranean and Other Poems (1936)

The Anabasis
The Ancestors
Fragment of a Meditation
To the Lacedemonians
The Meaning of Life
The Meaning of Death
The Mediterranean
Aeneas at Washington
Pastoral
The Robber Bridegroom
To the Romantic Traditionists
Shadow and Shade
Sonnets at Christmas (1934)
Unnatural Love

The Winter Sea (1944)

Eclogue of the Liberal and the Poet
False Nightmare
Jubilo
More Sonnets at Christmas (1942)
Ode to Our Young Pro-Consuls of the Air
Seasons of the Soul
The Trout Map
Winter Mask to the Memory of W. B. Yeats

"The Vigil of Venus" was published in the United States in a limited edition in 1943. The version of "Ode to the Confederate Dead" in the present collection appeared in *Selected Poems* (New York, 1937).

INDEX OF TITLES